ROADS OF HURT AND HOPE

OTHER BOOKS BY ANDREW D. MAYES

spiritualityadviser.com

Celebrating the Christian Centuries (1999)

Spirituality of Struggle: Pathways to Growth (2002)

Spirituality in Ministerial Formation (2009)

Holy Land? Challenging Questions from the Biblical Landscape (2011)

Beyond the Edge: Spiritual Transitions for Adventurous Souls (2013)

Another Christ: Re-envisioning Ministry (2014)

Learning the Language of the Soul (2016)

Journey to the Centre of the Soul (2017)

Sensing the Divine (2019)

Gateways to the Divine: Transformative Pathways of Prayer from the Holy City of Jerusalem (2020)

Diving for Pearls: Exploring the Depths of Prayer with Isaac the Syrian (2021)

Voices from the Mountains: Forgotten Wisdom for a Hurting World from the Biblical Peaks (2021)

Climate of the Soul: Ecological Spirituality for Anxious Times (2022)

Reforesting the Soul: Meditating with Trees (2022)

Treasure in the Wilderness: Desert Spirituality for Uncertain Times (2023)

ROADS OF HURT AND HOPE

Transformative Journeys in the Holy Land

ANDREW D. MAYES

RESOURCE *Publications* · Eugene, Oregon

ROADS OF HURT AND HOPE
Transformative Journeys in the Holy Land

Resource Publications
An Imprint of Wipf and Stock Publishers
199 W. 8th Ave., Suite 3
Eugene, OR 97401

www.wipfandstock.com

PAPERBACK ISBN: 979-8-3852-0957-6
HARDCOVER ISBN: 979-8-3852-0958-3
EBOOK ISBN: 979-8-3852-0959-0

VERSION NUMBER 01/10/24

Contents

List of Images

1. Map of the Holy Land
2. Between Mounts Gerizim & Ebal: The Patriarchs' Way
3. Ancient Baptistery, Via Maris, Gaza. Discovered at Jabaliya Refugee Camp 1999, destroyed 2023
4. Desert Road, Wadi Qelt, Judean Desert
5. Via Dolorosa, Jerusalem
6. Helping one another on Roman Road near Moza

PHOTOS - CREDITS

1. Brian Gotts Wikimedia Commons
2. Yair Dov, https://commons.wikimedia.org/wiki/File:%D7%94%D7%A8_%D7%A2%D7%99%D7%91%D7%9C_%D7%95%D7%94%D7%A8_%D7%92%D7%A8%D7%99%D7%96%D7%99%D7%9D_.jpg
3. al-ain.com
4. author
5. author
6. author

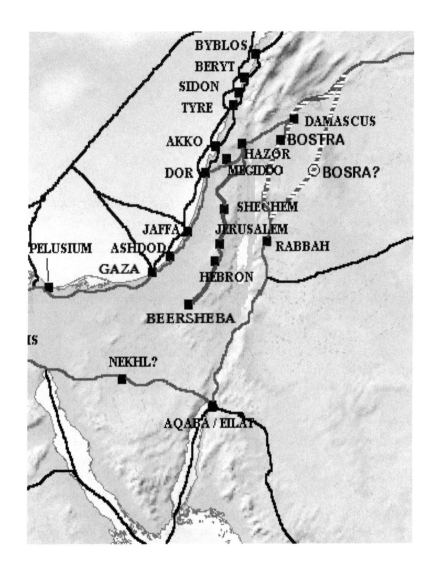

Map of the Holy Land

Introduction

Thus says the Lord: 'Stand at the crossroads, and look, and ask for the ancient paths, where the good way lies; and walk in it, and find rest for your souls' (Jer 6:16).

IN THIS COURSE WE become intrepid pilgrims, setting out on an adventure of faith, an odyssey of the soul. We revisit five biblical roads that have played such an influential role in our spiritual history. These ancient paths traversing ridge and valley, their stones full of biblical memories, are evocative of the travels of our ancestors in the faith and Jesus himself. We turn again to key scriptures as our guidebook for an unforgettable journey. But we also attend to contemporary voices: a wide range of short interviews immerses us in present-day realities. Thus the course is called *Roads of Hurt and Hope*.

But as we tread these roads across mountain, through desert, coastland and city, we realize their potential to challenge and change our perceptions, even the very course of our faith. They become *Transformative Journeys in the Holy Land*. We may never be the same again as we follow in the footsteps of Abraham, Jesus and courageous pilgrims, and as we allow ourselves to hear the cries of today's residents. Roads are about enabling movement. This book will help us along in our faith journey, open up to us new vistas and perspectives, and stimulate a movement in the soul, as perceptions shift, insights gained and challenges accepted.

ANCIENT PATHWAYS, PRESENT DANGERS

In Session 1, we tread in the hills of Samaria and Judea the Way of the Patriarchs and Matriarchs, leading south through Shechem/Nablus towards Jerusalem, and beyond to Hebron. We discover on this route used more than four millennia ago by the caravans of Abraham, Isaac and Jacob the development of unbreakable faith. This same road has been used by pilgrims to the Holy City through the centuries. The Romans developed and strengthened the road in their characteristic fashion, and their old curbstones and mile-stones are still to be found. From the roadside of today's troubled Route 60, we attend to those here who now strive to live lives of faith.

In Session 2, the Via Maris, the Way of the Sea, beckons us: "There will be no gloom for those who were in anguish . . . in the latter time he will make glorious the Way of the Sea, the land beyond the Jordan, Galilee of the nations . . . " (Isa 9:1). This ancient trade route between Egypt and Mesopotamia is in long stretches followed to this day by the modern Route 6 toll-road. We find it to be a road that calls us to solidarity with the hurting, as we pass Gaza venturing north into the heart of the Galilee region.

In Session 3 the traveler down the ancient Jordan Valley road passes Jericho via the Valley of Achor, which Hosea called "a door of hope" (Hos 2:15). After Jericho pilgrims to Jerusalem turn west: here the road climbs steeply, from over 850 feet below sea level to an altitude of 2600 feet at the Mount of Olives, reminding us that the Jewish word for pilgrim is *aliyah*, meaning "to go up": "Come let us go up to the house of the Lord" (Ps 122). The psalms of ascent (Pss 120–134) cheered pilgrims on their tough upward trek through the wilderness of Judea between Jerusalem and the Jordan; the ambush in the parable of the Good Samaritan (Luke 10:25–37) reminds us how dangerous this road could be. Indeed, it could be the "valley of the shadow of death" of the twenty third psalm, which discovers God's shepherd-like care in the midst of a dangerous route. We hear the road's call to risky compassion.

In Session 4 we walk the Via Dolorosa. As we rub shoulders with Mary, Simon of Cyrene and Veronica of old, we also encounter those living on this road today, and salute their indefatigable courage.

Session 5 invites us to walk the road to Emmaus, which leads us into the future fueled by an enduring, unbreakable hope.

USING THIS COURSE

This course is designed both for individual and group use. Participants will need their own copy. It can be used in Lent or at any time of year. The first three sessions have 6 elements, with suggested timings (sessions should last from an hour to an hour and half maximum) :

1. **Setting Out** – After a welcome (if in group) and opening prayer (at end of this introduction), we picture the scene, discovering the character of each road. (10 mins)

2. **Scripture** – this should be read aloud, if in a group, followed by a silence. (5 mins)

3. **Reflection** – the group leader gives a summary or precis of this, or asks group members what stands out for them, what strikes them and why. (15 mins)

4. **Voices from the Road** – this should be read aloud, so today's voices speak into our midst and can be heard. (10 mins)

5. **Questions** – for group discussion or individual consideration. The focus should be on identifying potential changes in oneself or discerning a course of action. (20 mins)

6. **Prayer Exercise** – if time permits, or use the final prayer provided. (10 mins)

The last two sessions are structured differently but contain all these elements.

BIBLICAL METAPHORS

Biblical writers utilize the image of the pathway or road as a metaphor for entering upon God's way of justice and salvation. Psalm 24 prays for guidance:

> Make me to know your ways, O Lord;
> Teach me your paths . . .
> He leads the humble in what is right,
> And teaches the humble his way.
> All the paths of the Lord are steadfast love and faithfulness (Ps 24:4,9, 10a)

The prophet Isaiah envisions a path to redemption: "A highway will be there, and it shall be called the Holy Way; the unclean shall not travel on it, but it shall be for God's people; no traveler, not even fools, shall go astray . . . but the redeemed shall walk there. And the ransomed of the Lord shall return, and come to Zion with singing . . . ." (35:8–10). The prophet hopes for the people's return from their exile, and sees the bleak desert becoming a "road of holiness" and a new exodus journey towards freedom.

This imagery is echoed by John the Baptist as he cries out: "prepare the way of the Lord, make his paths straight. Every valley shall be filled, and every mountain and hill shall be made low" (Luke 3: 3–6). John identifies closely with the landscape. As he looks out on the wild and precipitous cliffs and escarpments of the Judean wilderness, he can envision with Isaiah a levelling of the impossible natural barriers and the raising of new pathways to freedom. What was impassable and impenetrable becomes a gateway to a new future for God's people. John's message is that we need to open up in the landscape of our lives entry-points for the coming Messiah.

ROADS OF CONVERSION

In the Scriptures, the road is the place of encounter and conversion, and the place of surprise where the traveler must be open to unexpected happenings and people. While the mountains may represent strength and the ability to dominate landscape, embodied in the hilltop stronghold, the valleys are places of vulnerability and exposure. Many roads follow the valleys, but here travelers are prey to surprise attack: in the Old Testament Gideon's forces swoop down on the Midianite troops in the Jezreel valley (Judg 7:12ff) and the Philistines threaten David and his people in the valley of Elah (1 Sam 17:1, 17). The Arameans, sensing victory, jibed to the Israelites: "Your god is a god of the hills but he is not a god of the valleys!" (I Kgs 20:28). Unsuspecting travelers are attacked by marauding bandits. On the road, something good or bad can happen, and no one can foretell. A major theme in Mark's gospel is following Jesus along an unpredictable road: "They were on the road, going up to Jerusalem, and Jesus was walking ahead of them; they were amazed . . . " (10:32).

In John's gospel, the Samaritan woman is not expecting a Jewish traveler to pause and sit beside her, in the noon-day heat, at Jacob's Well, an important stopping place on the road through Samaria. She is not expecting him to ask her for a drink, and turn out to be "a man who told me everything I have ever done!" (John 4: 29). For her, this was a life-changing encounter with a Stranger. So too, the Ethiopian pilgrim, travelling on the road from Jerusalem to Gaza, was not bargaining on Philip to draw alongside him and to open to him the meaning of an enigmatic Scripture (Acts

8:26–40). This encounter led him into new faith in Jesus, sealed by baptism in waters beside the road. Saul truly finds the road to Damascus to be a place of conversion as he encounters the Risen Christ in a vision, when he was least expecting it (Acts 9:1–19): for him, Jesus was a dead man! Yet his encounter leads to a life-shattering experience, and an utterly new direction as he discovers a commission to be "apostle to the Gentiles." (It is significant that the Anglican Cathedral of St George, the seat of Archbishop Hosam Naoum and center of mission, is located on the Damascus Road in Jerusalem).

So today, the traveler on Holy Land roads must be prepared for the unpredictable and for the potential for conversion. There are hazards which cannot be foreseen: the erection of a new military checkpoint, the closure of a road. There are unexpected natural dangers: torrential flashfloods can sweep across the main road beside the Dead Sea when there is a downpour in Jerusalem! The floods gain momentum as they course through the narrow wadis or ravines of the Judean wilderness. There can be unexpected wildlife on the roads: camels, ibex or gazelles suddenly impeding the flow of traffic, or, overhead, the wondrous sight of flocks of migrating birds, large numbers of which make their passage from Europe to Africa over Israel. The roads in the Holy Land often open up the traveler to astonishing and breathtaking new vistas: as when the road through the Judean wilderness leads to a dramatic change of scenery upon reaching the wide Jordan rift valley, the mountains of Gilead and Moab rising majestically beyond the river, the stunning green oasis of Jericho promising refreshment after the desert. There can be unexpected glimpses of human settlements: new Israeli construction sites springing up, as it seems overnight, or the shanty-town tents of the Bedouin, sheep and goats herded nearby. Such experiences on the road sometimes come "out of the blue" for the pilgrim, and require what liberation theologians call "conversion to the neighbor": a new awareness of the plight of the oppressed, a readiness to confront pre-existing prejudices or perceptions.

This course originates from my ministry as course director and chaplain at St George's College Jerusalem. It complements my earlier book *Beyond the Edge: Spiritual Transitions for Adventurous Souls* which followed Jesus in his journeys across borders into liminal terrain that becomes life-changing. I hope this present offering will take the reader on transformative journeys too, in these uncertain times. The course was written in October and November 2023, during the Gaza war.

God of our pilgrimage,
as we walk these roads
lead us forwards in faith.
Be our companion on the road,
and make yourself known to us
through Jesus Christ our Lord, Amen.

Between Mounts Gerizim & Ebal: The Patriarchs' Way

1

The Way of the Patriarchs and Matriarchs

Forging Adventurous Faith

1 SETTING OUT

Today undoubtedly one of the most dangerous roads in the world, the north-south Route 60 through the Judean and Samarian highlands of the West Bank traces the path of Abraham and Sarah; Isaac and Rebekah, and Jacob and Rachel also probably passed this way. Abraham and Sarah, used to the flat plains of Mesopotamia beside the River Euphrates, found that this then stony road opened up astonishing new vistas as they followed its track south. Called the Ridge Route, it follows the watershed of the mountains, with the coastal strip to the west descending to the Mediterranean Sea, and the Judean wilderness dropping away to the deep Jordan valley to the east. This is the spine of the country. The limestone mountains have a raw beauty. Ancient terraces hug the contours of the steep rocky hillsides, redeeming a barren landscape: vines grow in the southern part and ageless olive groves are everywhere, silvery leaves glistening and shimmering in the sunlight. Ancient biblical towns punctuate the route: north of Jerusalem the road follows a pass between Mount Gerizim and Mount Ebal at Shechem (Nablus). Towards the south, it links Bethlehem, Hebron and

Beersheva. It was a risky route for Abraham and Sarah – with demanding rocky terrain and unknown dangers.

Since this region has been under military occupation for more than fifty years, today's traveler must be prepared for flashpoints where flare-ups of violence burst out, pitching Israeli settlers against Palestinian: south of Shechem, settlers recently destroyed part of the Arab village of Huwara which sits astride the road, while in Hebron stone throwing and worse is a daily feature of life in the divided town. Since 7 October 2023, settlers, supported by soldiers, have destroyed more than 3,000 olive trees in the area, and prevent Arab farmers from reaching their groves to harvest their precious annual crop. Normally, Route 60 sees a procession of trucks bearing olives to market or processing at this time of year, but today the road sees none. From this road branch off settler-only roads, barred to Palestinians: they slice through the landscape and divide up the terrain. Sacred land has become scarred, scared land.

John's gospel suggests that a divine imperative motivated Jesus to pass through this no-go area:

> Jesus left Judea and started back to Galilee. But he *had* to go through Samaria. So he came to a Samaritan city called Sychar, near the plot of ground that Jacob had given to his son Joseph. Jacob's well was there, and Jesus, tired out by his journey, was sitting by the well. (John 4;3–5)

In fact, in order to make a journey from Jerusalem to Galilee, Jesus had the choice of three possible routes. There was the Via Maris, the magnificent Roman Road that followed the coastal plain, the main trade route indeed from Egypt to Mesopotamia. This was an undemanding road, favored by traders and merchants, which we will tread in the next chapter. A second option followed the Jordan Valley. There one could walk in the great rift valley within sight of the River itself. But the third route was tricky and unpopular, for it passed through the Samaritan territory. It was physically difficult in places, because these central highlands of the country are characterized by steeply-sided hills and meandering ravines. Indeed, a valley south of Shechem is called, to this day, the Valley of the Thieves, because historically it was a place of ambush and attack. But of course this third route was undesirable from a Jewish point of view, because, as John reminds us, "Jews have no dealings with Samaritans." In Jewish eyes, Samaritans were hated pariahs, half-castes, religiously impure and to take this route would defile and contaminate the Jewish traveler. They were a despised underclass, a bastard people ever since the Assyrian deportation of the population in 722BC and the subsequent repopulating of the area with people of different bloods. Jews looked upon Samaritans with disdain. Samaria had become a hostile, no-go area. However, John tells us: "he *had* to go through Samaria" (John 4:3,4). Why did he *have* to take this route? What divine imperative impelled Jesus to choose this most treacherous way? Jesus wanted the disciples to have the experience of travelling through liminal terrain where they would be profoundly changed. Jesus was insistent on this passage to Galilee because he wanted his disciples to enter marginal, despised territory where many of their most cherished ideas about God and humanity would be shattered and reconstructed. Maybe, too, Jesus wanted to walk in the footsteps of Abraham and Sarah!

2 SCRIPTURE

> Now the Lord said to Abram, "Go from your country and your kindred and your father's house to the land that I will show you. I will make of you a great nation, and I will bless you, and make your name great, so that you will be a blessing. In you all the families of the earth shall be blessed."
>
> So Abram went, as the Lord had told him. Abram was seventy-five years old when he departed from Haran. Abram took his wife Sarai and his brother's son Lot, and all the possessions that they had gathered, and the persons whom they had acquired in Haran; and they set forth to go to the land of Canaan. When they had come to the land of Canaan, Abram passed through the land to the place at Shechem, to the oak of Moreh. From there he moved on to the hill country on the east of Bethel, and pitched his tent, and there he built an altar to the Lord and invoked the name of the Lord. And Abram journeyed on by stages towards the Negev. (Gen 12:1–9)

> Now faith is the assurance of things hoped for, the conviction of things not seen . . . By faith Abraham obeyed when he was called to set out for a place that he was to receive as an inheritance; and he set out, not knowing where he was going. By faith he stayed for a time in the land he had been promised, as in a foreign land, living in tents, as did Isaac and Jacob, who were heirs with him of the same promise. For he looked forward to the city that has foundations, whose architect and builder is God. By faith he received

power of procreation, even though he was too old—and Sarah herself was barren.

All of these confessed that they were strangers and foreigners on the earth, for people who speak in this way make it clear that they are seeking a homeland. If they had been thinking of the land that they had left behind, they would have had opportunity to return. But as it is, they desire a better country, that is, a heavenly one. Therefore God is not ashamed to be called their God; indeed, he has prepared a city for them.

By faith Abraham, when put to the test, offered up Isaac. He who had received the promises was ready to offer up his only son. (Heb 11:1, 8–11, 13–17)

3 REFLECTION

Seek Openness to the Divine

On this road, Abraham emerges, first and foremost as a person of unbreakable faith. Abraham becomes "the ancestor of all who believe" (Rom 4:11). He is astonishingly open to the Divine, even when God utters or commands things that are puzzling, unfathomable, seemingly impossible. "What then are we to say was gained by Abraham, our ancestor according to the flesh? . . . For what does the scripture say? 'Abraham believed God, and it was reckoned to him as righteousness'" (Rom 4:1,3). Abraham believed the promise of a son though such a birth was inconceivable in every sense. He was even willing to offer Isaac, the son of promise, when God demanded it (Heb 11:17–19). The kind of faith that Abraham models for us is unconditional trust and total availability to God – involving an ability to listen to God, to discover the Divine, open to surprises and to the unexpected. Abraham calls out to us across four millennia: "rule nothing out – if you seek the Divine!"

Keep a Pilgrim Heart

He was prepared to move – physically and spiritually. Genesis 12 tells us "Now the Lord said to Abram, "Go from your country and your kindred and your father's house to the land that I will show you." He was prepared to quit his comfort zone, leave behind his home, and venture forth on a journey into the unknown. He was prepared to let go of his familiar securities, even his cherished inherited concepts of God, and move out on a journey of faith: "he set out, not knowing where he was going" (Heb 11:8). Abraham truly had a pilgrim heart, or as the English poet of the 17th century from the Anglican tradition, George Herbert, put it: "a heart in pilgrimage." He was prepared to live with vulnerability, provisionality and risk, quitting his comfortable stone house, ready to be "living in tents" (Heb 11:9).

Wearied by his journey, Abraham and Sarah, together with their caravan, see the mighty oak standing proud in the landscape as they pass through the valley between Mount Gerizim and Mount Ebal. It becomes a destination to aim for and turns out to be a place of significant encounter with the Divine. Abraham pauses at the Oak of Moreh and makes this feature in the landscape both a staging-post and a place of worship and sacrifice: "He built an altar there." The Oak of Moreh at Shechem in the Canaanite highlands marks the point of arrival in the promised land and it is beneath its bowers that he experiences some kind of theophany: "the Lord appeared to Abram." The roadside tree marks a significant meeting with God and the first time God promises Abraham the gift of land for himself and his descendants.

Today we begin have a journey, we have set out together, we are beginning to move. With Abram and Sarah we step out into the unknown. We must be prepared, like Abraham himself, to let go sometimes of conventions and concepts that would pull us back and tie us down. We must be prepared, as it were, to "live in tents" – to live with the provisional, the impermanent, the uncomfortable, the unsettling, for as long as it takes. We do not know the outcome of our journey, but God does. God calls us to keep moving forwards as companions on the journey. Let us pray for the faith of Abraham to grow in our own hearts, an unshakable trust in God, the God of our pilgrimage.

"Walk Before Me"

> When Abram was ninety-nine years old, the Lord appeared to Abram, and said to him, "I am God Almighty; walk before me, and be blameless." (Gen 17:1)

As Abraham and Sarah walked along this highland track, what did they encounter on the road?

- They enjoyed a season of rest by the oaks of Mamre at Hebron (Gen 13:18)

- Abraham encountered Melchizedek (14:18)

- He met with God in a mysterious night-time encounter (15:12–21)

- God gave him a new name and a new destiny (17:1–8)

- Abraham and Sarah welcomed angels at Mamre (18:1–15)

- His faith was tested to the limit in the binding of Isaac (22:18)

- At Beersheva he faced conflict with Abimelech but found a path to reconciliation (21: 22–34)

4 VOICES FROM THE ROAD

I talked (November 2023) with a young priest Fr H serving a church in Nablus. Some details are changed to protect anonymity.

> First of all, the situation is now totally different to the time of Jesus, when he walked freely along this road and talked freely with the woman at the well. Sure, at that time, there were tensions between peoples – Jews and Samaritans. But today we can't move freely between Jerusalem and Jacob's Well. Route 60 is blocked. Today, if you want to walk the ancient route, it is very difficult to follow it. It is very difficult to walk in the footsteps of Jesus, where he moved.
>
> We need a heavenly faith and way of thinking, not earthly. It's important to get to the right meaning of what Jesus is asking us to do – to love. We use that word "love" in different ways – we say "I love food", meaning "I want food." But faith tells us, that in God's eyes, to love God and people is to give and not to take (like we do with food!). God asks us to reflect his image on this road – to speak of eternal life. God asks me to live this eternal life here, now, in this land. As Palestinian Christians we should love this place, and take care of it, because we have a mission to reflect God here. To walk with God's heart, to reflect his image as we meet people.
>
> So Route 60 now, in Nablus, and most of the roads around Nablus are blocked. Settlers come down and shoot us, and throw stones. I experienced it in my family two weeks ago. We needed to go north to get an urgent vaccine. But it is so complicated to cross borders. There are checkpoints everywhere now. Every road block we manage to cross is like achieving something great, because it

is not an easy job. Every stage is difficult – to pass along without clashes, without getting hurt.

We encourage people to pray for peace and hope. The prophets, and Jesus himself, faced terrible times – that encourages us. As believers, we accept that in this world you will have terrible moments. Jesus gave out peace and healing, and they gave him the gift of a cross in return. We accept the fact that the Bible does not promise us a road of flowers. I encourage myself by recalling the story of Job in the Old Testament – how he lost his family, his ten children – they died from a collapsing house. Today in Gaza entire families face this. But Job, all the time – while losing family and friends and animals – he kept his trust in God. That is real faith. Not blaming God for bad things but rather accepting that God is the only one who can help us change bad things.

What can we do? The children are on my heart. I dream of a program that can help the kids in kindergarten, and older ones – to help them overcome their traumas and nightmares. I want them to experience a culture of life, not death where they read on their mobiles about 10,000 dead. I dream of our teachers able to make healing for the kids, activities to take them out of the death zone. We want to support and show solidarity by helping people. We have an unused rooms by the church that could become a place where young people could get support, through cultural things like music, singing, arts, making pictures.

Prayer is most important right now. Prayer that our ministry can really make a difference – both our work with kids and in our local hospital. Prayer can move mountains. It can turn things upside down. Prayer changes things. It touches our hearts and minds. *Ya'ni,* you see, when we pray, we feel we want to do something more.

It is so difficult for Nablus right now – shootings, invasions into the Old City, killing people. I hear children of five or six years old singing songs for the martyrs. We don't want this culture of death for the kids. My faith makes me believe that they *can* have a beautiful life.

Fr H ends by talking about faithfulness, steadfastness in the face of daily trails, expressed in the Arabic word *sumud.* This means never giving up. Not giving in to despair. Staying determined. Not being worn down by fear. It expresses the heart of faith:

> *Sumud* is a great word we use: it means "keeps going". It reminds us we belong to this place and we should stay. If we abandoned

this road, it would stick forever in our heart. *Sumud* is a beautiful word that helps us understand faith here. Holding on.

One can support episcopal parishes on the West Bank via the American Friends of the Episcopal Diocese of Jerusalem or via Jerusalem and the Middle East Church Association (UK); Friends of the Holy Land supports Christians across the traditions.

Maybe, in all our human journeys infused with the Divine, wherever we tread, we face a mixture of faith and fear. Which will win out?

5 QUESTIONS

1. What do Abraham and Sarah teach us about the nature of faith?

2. In what ways is your faith tested?

3. How is your faith strengthened?

4. How is your faith revealed?

5. How does the voice from the road challenge you?

6 PRAYER EXERCISE

> *Abram journeyed on by stages (Gen 12:9, NRSV)*
> *Then he moved on toward the Negev, stopping for a time at several places on the way. (ERV)*

This exercise invites you to celebrate the stages and seasons of your life journey.

On a clean piece of paper (landscape) draw a personal "timeline" to recall the transitions you have faced in your life.

Draw a horizontal line and mark it into the decades of the road of your life. It might be a wavy line, rather than a straight one!

Above the line, marking with a cross, note and label major events and transitions, including new jobs, house-moves, births and deaths, new ministries – including "public" events recognized and shared by others.

Below the line, in the hidden section of the road as it were, note how you felt personally at these moments of change. How did you experience God at these times? How was your faith challenged or deepened?

Conclude by giving thanks for God's presence and providence in your life, and for your own journey of faith.

If in a group setting, you might like to reflect on this with a partner.

**Almighty and everlasting God, increase in us your gift of faith
that, forsaking what lies behind and reaching out to that which
is before,
we may run the way of your commandments
and win the crown of everlasting joy;
through Jesus Christ your Son our Lord.**

Ancient Baptistery, Via Maris, Gaza. Discovered at Jabaliya Refugee Camp 1999, destroyed 2023

2

Via Maris, Way of the Sea
Establishing Solidarity with the Hurting

1 SETTING OUT

With the shrieks of merchants and the clattering of hooves and creaking wheels on worn, ancient flagstones – the Via Maris at the time of Christ was a vibrant, noisy and colorful road. Fragrant, too – bearing caravans of camels and donkeys and wagons laden with spices and incense from as far afield as Africa. Today Israel's Route 4 and Route 6, a toll road, follow the course of this well-trodden track; further south, on the Gaza Strip, the venerable road is, as I write, a battlefield filled with tanks. The ancient trade route, dating from the early Bronze Age, linked Egypt with the northern empires of Syria, Anatolia and Mesopotamia — along the Mediterranean coast of modern-day Egypt, Gaza Strip, Israel and Syria. The coastal strip, lashed by foaming waves to its west and bounded by rugged highlands to its east, is 25 miles wide at Gaza, narrowing to 3 miles at the Lebanese border. *Via Maris* means "Way of the Sea", a phrase deriving from Isaiah 9:1. Indeed, it was the most important route from Egypt to Syria and the Fertile Crescent. Following the northern coast of Sinai through el-Arish and Rafah, it passed through Gaza, Ashkelon and Caesarea, before turning east through Megiddo and the Jezreel Valley until it reached Tiberias on the Sea of Galilee. Following the northern shore of the lake, its busy traffic brushed past Capernaum. Matthew at his tax booth (Matt 9:9–13) was collecting tolls and dues on merchandise from passing traders, for Capernaum was a border town marking the boundary between the district ruled by Herod Antipas and the tetrarchy of Phillip. It had its own garrison, for the centurion tells us "I am a man under authority, with soldiers under me" (Matt 8:9). Thence the road branched north east, climbing over the Golan Heights towards Damascus.

Gaza grew as a vital hub on this great trunk road, prospering by its junction with routes from Jerusalem and from across the Negev desert. Over its 4000 years, it thrived as a cosmopolitan city and center of commerce, learning and philosophy. Throughout the Roman period, and at the time of Christ, Gaza maintained its wealth, receiving grants from several different emperors. A 500-member senate governed the city, which had a diverse population of Greeks, Romans, Jews, Egyptians, Persians and Nabateans. Conversion to Christianity in the city was spearheaded by St Porphyrius, who destroyed its eight pagan temples between 396 and 420 AD. Hilarion (291–372) had already been pioneering the lifestyle and disciplines of the solitary life, and Gaza flourished as an early center of monastic life under Isaiah of Scetis (d 491), Barsanuphius (d 545) and Dorotheos (510–620).

The road, known today locally as Salah al Din Road, has been the life-blood of the city of Gaza, and indeed, the main reason for its existence. In 2010 Cunningham wrote: "Now, toiling farmers, tinkering mechanics and an array of colourful roadside businesses span the length of Salah al Din, from central to southern Gaza. Camels weave aimlessly between its lanes, workers dig for gravel at its edges, and teetering, horn-blaring lorries run up and down the road to ferry smuggled goods and aid assistance to Gaza's 1.5 million people ..." As I write today, in November 2023, it is strewn with bullet-riddled bodies which refugees must pass as they seek passage to the southern area of the Gaza strip. The church of St Porphyrius, Gaza's oldest, was destroyed by a direct missile strike on 19 October 2023, and it is feared that soon there will be no Christians left in this area where Christianity began.

Capernaum had a population of 2000 at the time of Christ. In his classic *In the Steps of the Master* H. V. Morton observes:

> In the time of Jesus the Sea of Galilee was one of the busiest centers of life in the country. His ministry was conducted not only in the most cosmopolitan region, but also in a territory where the ancient trade routes from Tyre and Sidon on the west, and the old

caravan roads from Damascus on the north-east, as well as the great imperial highways met together and branched out over the country. Galilee was on the main road of the ancient world, a half-way house between Damascus and the Egyptian frontier, on the one hand, and between Antioch and Jerusalem on the other.

When Jesus walked the roads of Galilee He met the long cara-vans working southward across the fords of Jordan. He saw the sun gleam on the spears of Roman maniples and cohorts. He met bands of Phoenician merchants travelling into Galilee; encoun-tered the litters and chariots of the great, and saw the bands of strolling players and jugglers and gladiators bound for the Greek cities of the Decapolis.

Jesus, walking the roads of Galilee, is walking the modern road, with its money-changers and tax-collectors, its market places and its unhappy rich men. He had chosen to live among people of many nations and upon one of the main highways of the Roman Empire.

Today, Gaza is noisy, not with the cries of merchants and traders, but with the sound of devastating bombs. Meanwhile, Capernaum and the northern shore of the Sea of Galilee is silent, except for the chatter of pilgrims and for the liturgies of the religious communities who welcome visitors to this section of the Via Maris.

2 SCRIPTURE

Then an angel of the Lord said to Philip, "Get up and go towards the south to the road that goes down from Jerusalem to Gaza." (This is a wilderness road.) So he got up and went. Now there was an Ethiopian court official, who had come to Jerusalem to wor-ship and was returning home; seated in his chariot, he was reading the prophet Isaiah. Then the Spirit said to Philip, "Go over to this chariot and join it." So Philip ran up to it and heard him reading the prophet Isaiah. He asked, "Do you understand what you are reading?" He replied, "How can I, unless someone guides me?" And he invited Philip to get in and sit beside him. Now the passage of the scripture that he was reading was this:

> "Like a sheep he was led to the slaughter, like a lamb silent before its shearer,
> so he does not open his mouth. In his humiliation justice was denied him.

Who can describe his generation? For his life is taken away from the earth."

The eunuch asked Philip, "About whom, may I ask you, does the prophet say this, about himself or about someone else?" Then Philip began to speak, and starting with this scripture, he proclaimed to him the good news about Jesus. As they were going along the road, they came to some water; and the eunuch said, "Look, here is water! What is to prevent me from being baptized?" He commanded the chariot to stop, and both of them, Philip and the eunuch, went down into the water, and Philip baptized him. When they came up out of the water, the Spirit of the Lord snatched Philip away; the eunuch saw him no more, and went on his way rejoicing. But Philip found himself at Azotus, and as he was passing through the region, he proclaimed the good news to all the towns until he came to Caesarea. (Acts 8:26–40)

Leaving Nazareth, he went and lived in Capernaum, which was by the lake in the area of Zebulun and Naphtali—to fulfill what was said through the prophet Isaiah:

> "Land of Zebulun and land of Naphtali, the Way of the Sea, beyond the Jordan, Galilee of the Gentiles—
> the people living in darkness have seen a great light;
> on those living in the land of the shadow of death a light has dawned."

From that time on Jesus began to preach, "Repent, for the kingdom of heaven has come near." Jesus went throughout Galilee, teaching in their synagogues, proclaiming the good news of the kingdom, and healing every disease and sickness among the people. News about him spread all over Syria, and people brought to him all who were ill with various diseases, those suffering severe pain, demon-possessed, those having seizures, and the paralyzed; he healed them. (Matt 4:12–17, 23)

3 REFLECTION

Gaza, the once-thriving center of commerce, culture and civilization on the Via Maris, with its important witness to Christian faith has become in our day the world's largest open-air prison, the Gaza Strip home to two million people crowded into an area of 140 square miles. No through passage

is possible, for Gaza City and its Strip is under miliary and economic block-
ade. It is wracked by chronic unemployment, contaminated drinking water,
few hours of electricity, and ever-rising tensions that reached boiling point
in October 2023, when in response to attacks on Israel it was bombed almost into oblivion.

The discovery made by the Ethiopian traveler on the road seems more
apposite than ever. He discovered not a remote antiseptic deity locked up
in a faraway heaven, but a dusty, bleeding God who is with us, among us, in
our trials. He was reading one of Isaiah's Servant Songs that also contained
the words:

> He was despised and rejected by others;
>   a man of suffering and acquainted with infirmity;
> and as one from whom others hide their faces
>   he was despised, and we held him of no account.
> Surely he has borne our infirmities and carried our diseases;
>   yet we accounted him stricken, struck down by God, and
> afflicted.
> But he was wounded for our transgressions, crushed for our
> iniquities;
>   upon him was the punishment that made us whole,
>   and by his bruises we are healed. (Isa 53:3–5)

Philip helped him to see that these ancient words pointed to a Savior who
is "God is with us" in our greatest pain – a God who weeps among us in
deepest solidarity with the human condition.

This too is the meaning of Matthew's description of Jesus following
the Via Maris into the pain of Galilee.

On what grounds does Galilee acquire this designation "Galilee of the
Gentiles"? Is it a compliment or an insult? The phrase means literally: "circle
of pagans." The Galilee region was much more mixed in terms of Jewish and
Gentile populations than other regions of the land. A semi-autonomous
frontier region, it was exposed to the nearby foreign countries and eth-
nicities. It found itself on the edges. Galileans were mocked for their local
accent – recall the girl's recognition of Peter's rough Aramaic tongue – they
were jeered at and scapegoated. "Search and you will see that no prophet
is to arise from Galilee" (John 7:52). Lee in his book *From a Liminal Place*
observes:

> Galileans were not just left alone in their liminal situation but
> were oppressed, dehumanized and looked down upon. Galileans

were marginalized by foreign invaders and also by the Jerusalem Temple-state...Galilee was repeatedly invaded and exploited by foreign empires throughout its history.

But above all, it was a place of deep poverty and need. The Galileans were crippled by heavy taxes, dues were owed to the Roman occupier, and Temple taxes added to the burden. At the time of Jesus ordinary families were being forced to quit their ancestral landholdings, where they had lived for centuries, in order to meet these demands. Land was also confiscated for the building projects and villas of the urban elite at Sefforis and Tiberias. But then they had to pay rent for what had been their fields and homes: they became caught in a downwards economic spiral, becoming tenants in their own property. We should note how many of Jesus' parables speak of absentee landlords who impose severe dues on their tenants (see, for example, Luke 16:1–8; Matt 25:14–30). Tax and rent robbed the Galilean peasant farmer of two thirds of the family income. Many were living at barely subsistence level.

No doubt Matthew preserves an original aspect of the Lord's Prayer when he puts it: "Forgive us our debts and we forgive those who are in debt to us" (Matt 6:12). Jesus asks his disciples to pray for the coming of God's Kingdom. This is a subversive prayer when taught and uttered in the context of first century Galilee, for it embodies a challenge to the prevailing kingdom, the kingdom of Rome, the rule of the Caesar. But this imperial reign had become stiflingly oppressive for the Galilean. The area of Galilee became a base for resistance to Rome's occupation, and the seedbed of the Zealot movement. The Gospels mention several times the designation *lestes* (eg. Mark 14:48, 15:27), which we translate "thieves" but really denotes social bandits. Josephus tells us about revolutionary activists in Galilee who sought to undermine Roman domination by acts of sabotage or terrorism: the precursors of the Jewish Zealots and Sicarri. Where there is oppression amidst powerlessness, one reaction is the rise of violent terrorists or guerrilla fighters. We will meet *lestes* again, on the desert road between Jerusalem and Jericho in the next session. Ever since the uprising by the Judas the Galilean in 4BC, Galilee was infamous for these protesters and rebels. Galilee had become a place of oppression and protest, populated by the poor, the broken and hurting, the rejected and stigmatized.

It is significant that Jesus did not base his ministry in quiet Nazareth, a remote village of 200 tucked away in the hills, but in Capernaum, with a population of 2000, on the Via Maris, alongside the crushed and the wounded. Despite benefiting from its favorable location on the trade route, Capernaum itself also knew first-hand situations of injustice and dehumanization in the region. Jesus comes to share their pain, and bring into it a better way: the Kingdom of God, where every human life is honored and cherished.

To follow Jesus to Galilee demands that we linger on the edge of the Church, alert and responsive to those who are just beginning their spiritual quest. And it demands that we position ourselves on the edge of society, on the fringes, among the confused and searching.

Jesus awaits us in the Galilee-like populations of our own time. He is already there: he does not need to be brought there. He is there, and we will always be catching up with him. He indeed, is the forerunner, the pioneer, the precursor: he gets there before we do. But he waits for us to greet him and honor him in the poor and marginalized, and to recognize his features in the faces of those who suffer. In the gospels the Risen Christ instructs us to go beyond borders, and to reach across frontiers. Matthew's gospel ends with the Great Commission: "Go therefore and make disciples of all nations" (28:19). The Greek *ethnos* denotes nations or different peoples. We are to get ourselves across the boundaries, over frontiers. But we are not alone in the venture: "remember, I am with you always, to the end of the age" (Matt 28:19).

4 VOICES FROM THE ROAD

On the path of the Via Maris is Ramla (Ramleh, near Lod/ Lydda).

Ramla flourished through the centuries as the junction between the north-south Via Maris and the east-west road from Jerusalem to the port of Jaffa: it was the commercial center of Palestine, thriving as a hub for pottery, dyeing, weaving, and olive oil, an Arab town until 1948. Then Israeli forces removed the Arab population in ethnic cleansing and repopulated the houses with newly arrived Jewish immigrants, fleeing the Europe that permitted the Holocaust and extermination camps. Dalia Landau was a small child when her parents brought her to newly-founded Israel in 1948 from Bulgaria. The family was assigned one of the former Arab homes, newly emptied: it had a lemon tree in the garden. Years passed, and one day a teenage lad showed up at Dalia's house, with a friend: Dalia, a teenager, was on her own, her parents were out. The Arab lad explained that this was his father's house – his father still had the key and told him that it was the one with the lemon tree outside– he just wanted to look around. Dalia welcomed him across the threshold: a friendship was formed.

After her parents died, and she inherited the house, Dalia opened it as a kindergarten where Jewish and Arab children could play together. She called it "Open House". The story is told in Sandy Tolan's *The Lemon Tree*. Dalia tells me:

> It is a challenge to stay with the pain of the mutual hurting between Palestinian Arab and Jew. You can either run away from it, deny it, or maybe it is truer to live with the pain – that opens possibilities of healing. What we all need is an open heart, that enables us to hear the reality of the Other. The open heart opens the way to miracles: we are supernatural beings, not natural! When we really listen – not having our prepared answers – we can overcome the negative energy that comes from prejudice.
>
> You can either picture Jerusalem – using biblical imagery – as bride or mother. A bride can have only one partner. But a mother, can give nurture to many.
>
> It all comes from the heart. We need to expand the heart, widen it: this can be a painful process and takes time. But Isaiah says, "enlarge the tent of your heart."

Near Capernaum, on the shore of Galilee lives a Benedictine Community.

Around the Sea of Galilee there are several Christian sites along the Via Maris. A Benedictine community looks after the Church of the Multiplication of the Loaves and the Fishes, and runs a guesthouse near the water's edge. The community consists of five German brothers and five Filipino sisters. Sister Layla speaks about their double ministry of welcome and encouragement.

> First of all, we are here to welcome weary pilgrims. We create a special atmosphere of prayer at here at Pilgerhaus which brings great refreshment to the spirit. In fact it renews people body and soul. But we also have a second ministry which few know about. Every weekend the sisters go down Route 6 to Tel Aviv to minister to the Filipino community there. You know that Filipino women work in many Israeli households. It is a very sacrificial life. Many

are mothers and have left their children with relatives back home thousands of miles away and try to send money there every month. They also worry that their husbands will take in other women while they are away. But I find that many of these Philippine workers are anxious, depressed and sometimes maltreated. So we have an important ministry of listening and support to them. The way I see it is this: living here at the edge of the lake trains us to be listeners for the Risen Christ. We drink in the silence here and we listen for his voice. But this is not something to be kept to ourselves like a private possession. It is a gift of listening and attentiveness to be shared. It is an experience which equips us for ministry. So we go each week to see the Filipino women. They pour out their hearts to us. They tell us about the pain they feel being separated from the children and loved ones. They tell us about bad employers and the worry they feel. You know, often they are hurting very much. We listen. We share what we have been given by the Risen Christ. I suppose it is like the Church of the Loaves and Fishes here. What you are given is to be shared, to meet the needs of the moment.

A Challenge from the Via Maris

Dorotheos (510–620), we noted, was one of the monastic pioneers who lived amidst the Gazan sands. Around 540 he founded his own monastery beside the road, going on to bequeath to us a large collection of teachings, *Discourses and Sayings: Directions on Spiritual Training*. Perhaps he has in mind the great trunk road of the spice route when he advises us to take stock:

> This is the King's highway of which one of the elders used to say, "Walk by the King's highway and count up the miles." This is the royal road by which all the saints travelled; the different states of the soul are the milestones by which a man has to pass – always looking to see where he is, how many miles he has covered and what a state he is in. So suppose we are all on the road, each one has a special objective there in the Holy City. And having left our own city some of us have covered five miles and turned back; some have gone ten, some have got half way there. Others perhaps have not even started on the journey, but have left the city and remain outside the gates on the evil-smelling rubbish dump. There are other travelers who, when they have gone a couple of miles, lose their way and retrace their steps; others travel two miles forward

and five miles backwards . . . that is how it is with us, for there are some among us who have left the world and came to the monastery with the intention of acquiring the virtues. Some keep straight on for a little, but do not persevere. Others make some progress, others have got half way then stand still . . .

Let each of us then take the trouble to find out where we are: whether we have left our own city but remain outside by the rubbish heap, or whether we have gone forward a little or much . . . Let each one find out about his own condition, the state of his soul; giving free rein to his passions, or checking them or uprooting them . . .

Let everyone then find out where he is; how many milestones he has passed on the road . . . May God, who is so good, shelter us from enemies, and give us self-control, and lead us forward on his road.

5 QUESTIONS

1. "Let everyone then find out where he is; how many milestones he has passed on the road." How would you describe your location, spiritually speaking? Name the milestones you have reached.

2. What impeded your progress? What advanced it?

3. How is it possible to deepen a sense of solidarity with people suffering some distance away?

4. How might such a solidarity be expressed or manifested? What are its implications for our lifestyle and personal priorities?

5. How do you experience the tension between being committed to your locality yet maintaining support for those in trial overseas? How can one maintain engagement with the locality while avoiding narrowing parochialism?

6. Philip was prepared to move by the Spirit to a seeker on the Gaza road, and Jesus was ready to relocate himself to Capernaum on the Via Maris for the sake of mission. How prepared are we to move, either physically or metaphorically, to get alongside the Other in pain?

7. What strikes you from the interviews about solidarity with the hurting?

6 PRAYER EXERCISE

Use the "cross-prayers" devised by Francis of Assisi.

1. Open your arms wide – extend them as far as you can. This is first to embody a solidarity with the cross. Think of Jesus opening wide his arms on the cross to embrace all who suffer, all who are in any form of distress. Think of Christ's all-encompassing love and acceptance. Make your outstretched arms a symbol of outreaching and enfolding love and concern.

2. Second, think of the Risen Christ and the way he longs to enfold the whole of creation, the little ones and marginalized ones of the earth.

3. Third, offer this prayer as an act of intercession. It is a prayer that hurts – in the sense that your arms will grow weary and ache. Moses prayed like this and had to have others hold his arms up (Exod 17:11,12). As you feel the ache, let it connect you to those who are in pain, those who are hurting: the sick, the dispossessed, those whose human rights are trampled on.

4. Finally, use this prayer-action as an act of self-offering. Offer yourself afresh to God for the part he has in store for you in his mission of reconciliation in the world.

> **God our Father,**
> **in love you sent your Son**
> **that the world may have life:**
> **lead us to seek him among the outcast**
> **and to find him in those in need,**
> **for Jesus Christ's sake.**

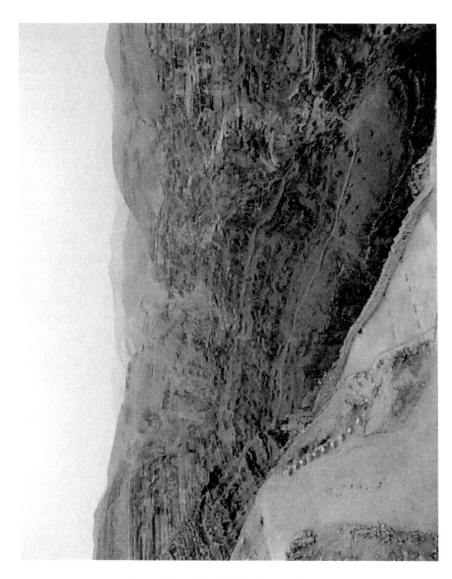

Desert Road, Wadi Qelt, Judean Desert

3

Road through Wilderness
Risking Insane Compassion

1 SETTING OUT

The treacherous road between Jerusalem's Mount of Olives (at 2600 feet) and Jericho (at 850 feet below sea level) passes through the Judean wilderness. There is no other way, and remnants of the Roman road are still to be found above the Wadi Qelt, the deep ravine that zigzags across this rocky desert landscape.

The Judean desert stretches east from the central highlands towards the fault-line scarp of the Great Rift Valley: a windswept, rocky and rugged wilderness where mountains, cliffs, and chalk hills tower above deeply-incised canyons. Scorched by shimmering heat, the chiseled ravines are parchingly dry for much of the year, but in winter, rains from Jerusalem pour through them in torrents forceful enough to move great boulders, which litter the riverbed. Acacia and juniper trees cling to the cliffs, while hawks circle overhead, Bedouin's goats picking their way gingerly over the rocks. The deep silence is broken only by the cry of birdsong, the tinkle of a goat bell, the whisper of the wind – and by the occasional clatter of a helicopter or screech of a jet, since this desert has been under military occupation since 1967, forming a significant portion of the West Bank.

The Judean desert is a place of paradox: rugged grandeur, raw splendor, untamable beauty, threatening yet inviting, affirming yet disturbing, a place of life and death. It was at the edge of these very hills that the Qumran community established itself about 100BC: later producing the Dead Sea Scrolls, they sought to model an alternative apocalyptic community awaiting the Redeemer. The desert has always attracted those on the social margin: fugitives, solitaries, outlaws, hermits, bandits . . .

The Wadi Qelt begins in the narrow ravine of the Wadi Faran, in the desert east of Jerusalem, where we find the very first Judean monastery, founded in 275 by St Chariton. Today, a sole Russian monk occupies this cave-complex. In the depths of the Wadi Qelt a small community resides at St George of Chobiza, while clinging precariously to the precipitous cliffs above Jericho is the Monastery of the Temptation of Christ. Near the Jordan River, five miles north of the Dead Sea, lies the Greek Orthodox monastery of St Gerasimos.

What did early western visitors make of this landscape? The Reverend Monro Vere trod the ruinous surface of the Roman road, mentioned in the parable of the Good Samaritan, in 1835 and relates in his *Summer Ramble in Syria*:

> The road passed close to Bethany . . . As we advanced, cultivation gradually lessened, and at last entirely disappeared. The road, after keeping the rocky tract at the top of the hill for a short time, descends into a valley or ravine; at the head of which is a fountain, said to have been frequently visited by the Apostles in passing from Jerusalem to Jericho . . . We reached a narrow pass cut in the mountain. The strata near it lie in arches, or in waves, or they are sometimes vertical; generally of oolite [limestone] . . . The descent was rough, abrupt, and extremely difficult; the view singularly wild; the parched and arid surface of the tract before us bore the aspect of extreme desolation.

As we turn to the New Testament, we discover that the Gospel actually begins in this very desert of human need, in this symbol of humanity's thirst for God: "The beginning of the good news of Jesus Christ, the Son of God. As it is written in the prophet Isaiah: 'See, I am sending my messenger ahead of you, who will prepare your way: the voice of one crying out in the wilderness: Prepare the way of the Lord!'" (Mark 1:1,2).

John the Baptist, perhaps standing on the Roman road above the wadi, longs for a highway to be opened up in the human heart. He finds inspiration in the prophet Isaiah:

> In the wilderness prepare the way of the Lord,
>   make straight in the desert a highway for our God.
> Every valley shall be lifted up,
>   and every mountain and hill be made low;
> the uneven ground shall become level,
>   and the rough places a plain.
> Then the glory of the Lord shall be revealed. (Isa 40:3~5)

John's voice echoes among the rocks and waste-places: "Turn back to God!" The desert, symbolic of humanity's emptiness, becomes the place of salvation, the place of transformation, through John's call to *metanoia*, repentance, a total re-orientation of human lives towards God. The Greek word *meta* means "beyond" or "big" while *noia* means "mind" – so the invitation is to go beyond our existing mindset, to go into the big mind, to allow ourselves, in the desert, to see things differently!

Soon Jesus enters the rocky canyons of the Judean wilderness, experiencing it as place of angels and wild beasts (Mark 1:13). The desert is a raw, wild, untamed place, calling forth authenticity and honesty from the soul. It is an eroded place, where the elements of wind and sun and water split rocks and crumble cliffs, symbolizing the brokenness of humanity. It is an open place, bespeaking of the vulnerability of the soul.

2 SCRIPTURE

Scholars affirm that the Wadi Qelt, below the Roman road from Jerusalem to Jericho, is the most likely setting of a familiar psalm:

> The Lord is my shepherd, I shall not want.
> He makes me lie down in green pastures;
> he leads me beside still waters; he restores my soul.
> He leads me in right paths for his name's sake.
> Even though I walk through the darkest valley,
> I fear no evil; for you are with me; your rod and your staff— they comfort me.
> You prepare a table before me in the presence of my enemies;
> you anoint my head with oil; my cup overflows.
> Surely goodness and mercy shall follow me all the days of my life,

and I shall dwell in the house of the Lord my whole life long.
(Psalm 23)

The Parable of the Good Samaritan is located on this road:

> Wanting to justify himself, the lawyer asked Jesus, "And who is my
> neighbor?" Jesus replied, "A man was going down from Jerusalem
> to Jericho, and fell into the hands of robbers, who stripped him,
> beat him, and went away, leaving him half dead. Now by chance a
> priest was going down that road; and when he saw him, he passed
> by on the other side. So likewise a Levite, when he came to the
> place and saw him, passed by on the other side. But a Samaritan
> while travelling came near him; and when he saw him, he was
> moved with pity. He went to him and bandaged his wounds, hav-
> ing poured oil and wine on them. Then he put him on his own
> animal, brought him to an inn, and took care of him. The next
> day he took out two denarii, gave them to the innkeeper, and said,
> "Take care of him; and when I come back, I will repay you what-
> ever more you spend." Which of these three, do you think, was a
> neighbor to the man who fell into the hands of the robbers?" He
> said, "The one who showed him mercy." Jesus said to him, "Go and
> do likewise." (Luke 10: 29–37)

3 REFLECTION

The parable confronts us with a choice of responses to acute human need,
represented in the bleeding, wounded, ambushed victim of violence.

The Priest and Levite, passing by on the other side, in fact represent
the religiously devout. They fail to respond to the victim of attack because
they can't do anything against their conventions of ritual purity: according to the rules they can't touch anything "half-dead". They have come, no
doubt, from the Jerusalem temple – purified, cleansed and forgiven – and
their priority is to uphold and protect their so-called holiness. They are not
being callous or indifferent in passing by – just being traditional, sensible
but constricted by religious rules. How often are we held back by sticking to
our respected, well-established inherited norms and routines, that nothing
may interrupt. Quiet – I am trying to pray! God doesn't want his people to
simply follow a list of rules; he's after the heart, and he wants his followers
to love others as he does.

"But a Samaritan while traveling came near him; and when he saw him, he was moved with pity." The word Jesus used for what the Samaritan felt toward the wounded man we translate as "compassion," a beautiful word; in Greek it means "pity from your deepest soul" – a love so deep-seated that it comes from your gut – in the older English "feeling the bowels of pity." It refers to the inner person, including the womb and the heart, both in a physical and metaphorical sense. This "gut-level compassion" is literally visceral. It is a response springing from raw feeling and basic humanity rather than from reason or thought, from instinct not logic. It comes from the depths.

The Samaritan didn't stop to calculate the cost and work out if it was within his budget or limitations of time. In fact he suspended his own agenda, set aside his own timetable and personal plans, and allowed himself to respond unhesitatingly and without caution or timidity. He set aside any inherited Samaritan prejudices against Jews that he himself might have harbored – "Jews have no dealings with Samaritans", as John 4 tells us – and vice versa! We could call this inner impulse, this irresistible imperative, a crazy compassion. It was costly, too. The cascading of wine and oil, poured into open wounds – plus the unstingy opening of the wallet – symbolize the reckless generosity of the man.

The Samaritan, of course, was a displaced person. He was faraway from his homeland. What was he doing there, in the Judean desert? Was he lost? He tells us, that even when we feel disorientated or confused, or "on a mission" about something, we can still be a channel of grace to those we come across, if we live in a spirit of availability. An insane compassion? Certainly ready to defy conventions, to express a certain extravagance in caring, to set aside the choking restrictions of "reasonable" living!

Living the same kind of life as Christ lived?

Jesus fuels and energizes such an unbridled response by the empowering grace of the Holy Spirit. Those who have experienced the gospel develop an uncontrollable impulse to be generous and a crazy ability to accept others in a Christ-like way. As 1 John 2:6 (JB) reminds us, "The one who claims to be living in him should be living the same kind of life as Christ lived." Christ invites us to live in freedom, responding with an unselfconscious, unpremeditated, spontaneous compassion springing from the heart.

As we travel through the gospels, we notice unconventional, provocative and prophetic actions by Jesus, so that his family thought he was insane (Mark 3:21). The Greek means literally "out of his mind." He comes eating and drinking. He picks wheat on the Sabbath day. He calls a child in the midst of the disciples to teach them about true greatness. He celebrates how God reveals the most important things to babies. In the midst of the storm on the lake, he falls asleep, his head on a cushion. He embraces the untouchable leper. He allows dubious women to anoint him, and dry him with their flowing hair.. He does enigmatic things, drawing in the dust. He walks on water and invites Peter to join him. He makes his solemn entry into Jerusalem seated on an ass! He is not too bothered about what other people might think. He just gets on with what is necessary.

Above all and through all, Christ wants us to be moved by a spontaneous love paying no attention to racial, religious or socioeconomic categories. God invites us to see beyond the exterior of lifestyle, color, and even religious affiliation to the divine image in everyone. The one who reached out to the Syrophoenician woman, the woman caught in adultery, the Samaritan woman by the well, the lepers on the roads in Samaritan lands (Luke 17:11–19) waits to meet us in the hungry, wounded, sick and imprisoned (Matt 25).

On the very same road Jesus reveals his way of responding. From the gutter comes a cry of help:

> As he and his disciples and a large crowd were leaving Jericho, Bartimaeus son of Timaeus, a blind beggar, was sitting by the roadside. When he heard that it was Jesus of Nazareth, he began to shout out and say, "Jesus, Son of David, have mercy on me! Let me see again."

Jesus responds with compassion, saying "Go; your faith has made you well." Poignantly, the account tells us:

> Immediately he regained his sight and followed him on the road. (Mark 10:46)

Bartimeus follows Jesus on the Roman road up to Jerusalem. It is Jesus' final journey. This road has become the entry point to the Way of the Cross.

Compassion Unlimited?

Perhaps we need to look again at the Parable of the Good Samaritan and ask different questions about those we call robbers but who are actually in the Greek text called *lestes* – freedom fighters – the designation, we noted in the last session, referring not to petty thieves but to social bandits, members of the protest movement against the oppression of Rome.

Indeed, Jesus himself is arrested in Gethsemane as one of these: 'Then Jesus said to them, "Have you come out with swords and clubs to arrest me as though I were a bandit?"' (Mark 14:48). On Calvary Jesus will be crucified between two freedom fighters: he takes his place among the *lestes*. according to Mark 15:27. Furthermore, on the cross Jesus extends compassion to the bandit beside him, promising "Truly I tell you, today you will be with me in Paradise" (Luke 23:43). There is a wideness in God's mercy: might even terrorists or guerrilla fighters find a place in heaven?

What desperation led the gang of *lestes* to attack the traveler on the road? Were they driven by sheer hunger? What oppressions were they facing that turned them into the role of *lestes*? We must not condone their brutal attack, but we can ask, should ask: what lay behind it? Can we, indeed, find room in our hearts to have compassion on their plight, and on the anguish and griefs of their wives and children? The One who treads this desert road that leads ultimately to Calvary and beyond, asks us to forgive and accept people without limit.

4 VOICES FROM THE ROAD

Ancient Voices

Very near the Roman road, a still living monastery in the Wadi Qelt was founded by St George of Choziba (d. 625), which he made a "place of hospitality" and "a shelter for the poor and visitors." Originally from Cyprus, he lived here for many years, including the testing time of the Persian invasion of 614. His biography composed by his disciple Antony reveals a semi-eremitical lifestyle balancing the demands of work and prayer, solitude and community: usually, except for times of persecution, George lived alone in his cell, coming to the cenobium on Saturdays and Sundays for fellowship and eucharist. His biography, translated in *Journeying into God,* tells us:

The old man [George as an elder] used to ask those who were cellarers at the time not to do the baking without him. For he said that it was an especially great reward to do such work in this holy place, for most of the bread was consumed by visitors. He also took on the ministry of the cisterns that were along the road to Jericho. He would help and work along with the gardeners, too, and willingly perform each ministry. He was eager to show great cooperation concerning the monastery's work on behalf of visitors, not only on account of the reward but also because he was eager to be an example for the brothers . . .

Our holy father George was sitting among the rocks, warming himself in the heat of the sun (for he was very thin on account of his abstinence). Boiling over with the desire of spiritual love to do the work that God wills, with fervent tears he was calling upon God, the lover of humankind, asking him to be merciful to his people.

We can all learn from the example of another of the monks – he remains anonymous – whom John Moschos heard about in 600 AD living near the road, related in his *Spiritual Meadow*:

When he went into the wilderness and settled at the Cells of Choziba this elder was greatly considerate of his neighbors. He would travel the road from the holy Jordan to the Holy City of Jerusalem carrying bread and water. And if he saw a person overcome by fatigue, he would shoulder that person's pack and carry it all the way to the holy Mount of Olives. He would do the same on the return journey if he found others, carrying their packs as far as Jericho. You would see this elder, sometimes sweating under a great load, sometimes carrying a youngster on his shoulders. There was even an occasion when he carried two of them at the same time. Sometimes he would sit down and repair the footwear of men and women if this was needed, for he carried with him what was needed for that task. To some he gave a drink of the water that he carried with him and to others he offered bread. If he found anyone naked, he would give him the very garment he wore. You saw him working all the day long.

Contemporary Bedouin Voice

Mohammed, in his fifties, has a sun-darkened weathered face, and is dressed in traditional robes protecting him from scorching sun and the fierce dust-bearing winds. He speaks to me (October 2023) above the Wadi Qelt, by the Roman road:

> We live in constant fear. Our brothers just north of here are attacked by settlers. Their homes are set on fire. Here in this valley we are harassed by the soldiers. We live in our black tents down in the valley. Every day is uncertain for us. It is uneasy. I try to stick to quietly shepherding my goats and selling things to tourists, when they come! They are not coming now. I try to keep my head down. But we Bedouin have to look out for each other. Down in the Jordan valley, just up from Jericho, our schools are regularly demolished. We make them of mudbrick, so we can rebuild! People are being moved off their lands, and structures built without permission are flattened. But it is difficult, very difficult. Will you buy a camel bone necklace? I wish someone would come and help us!

5 QUESTIONS

1. Is anything holding you back from risky compassion – "to give and not to count the cost" ? What is limiting your crazy, uncalculating response to human dilemma?

2. What does this parable say to you in relation to current human crises in the world?

3. How much compassion do you have for present-day *lestes*?

4. How does the parable challenge you to act differently?

5. What strikes you from the roadside voices, ancient and modern?

6 PRAYER EXERCISE

Use your hands expressively in this exercise.

Begin by clenching your fists tight and holding them before you. Feel the tension and let these fists represent an anger or frustration that bothers you today, a situation in the world that you feel strongly about or a person you care about facing some kind of stress. Hold them before God in the solidarity of prayer and intercession.

Second, slowly open your downturned palms and let go of the tension. Release your grip. Let it fall away from you to God. In this gesture, give to

God any negative feelings or stresses; feel them drip out of your fingertips, as it were. Surrender the situation to God's providence and sovereignty.

Third, turn your hands upwards in a gesture of surrender to God and of receiving from God. Recall the blessing God has given you in the receiving of Holy Communion in these palms. Breathe in his empowering Spirit, who gives you the courage for risky actions.

Finally, take a look at your hands. Feel the creases, their complexion; trace the lines. They witness to your unique human journey, with its mix of pleasure and pain. But now they are ready to reach out to others, to touch others. Is there an action that God is calling you to make in relation to your initial concern? What should you do as a result of your prayer – something bold, something risky or compassionate?

End with a prayer attributed to Ignatius of Loyola:

> **Teach us, good Lord,**
> **to serve you as you deserve,**
> **to give and not to count the cost,**
> **to toil and not to seek for rest,**
> **to labor and not to ask for any reward,**
> **save that of knowing that we do your will.**

Via Dolorosa, Jerusalem

4

Via Dolorosa, Way of the Cross
Encountering Indefatigable Courage

THE MOST FAMOUS ROAD in the Christian imagination, the Way of the Cross, the Via Dolorosa, is depicted on the walls of thousands of churches worldwide – after the Franciscans in the fourteen century popularized the devotion, and parish churches provided pictorial representations in the form of "The Stations" for those who could not go on pilgrimage to Jerusalem. Today it remains the most popular Lenten devotion and has spread beyond the Catholic Church to be adopted by a wide array of reformed churches.

Sometimes people are tempted to transform this into something too narrowly devotional, an individualistic matter between "me and my Lord", disconnected from contemporary realities in the wider world. Another risk is that it be limited to being an act of historical remembrance, as if only marking a faraway event, unrelated to the present. But there is a great opportunity to rediscover the Way of the Cross as one of the most powerful forms of intercession there is, as we allow it to lead us into prayerful solidarity with those who suffer on the face of the earth.

In this session, we meet those who actually live on the physical Via Dolorosa in Jerusalem today. It is a road marked by paradox. It is marked by heartache and hope, by desperation and ideology, by failure and promise. It is a street of anguish and aspirations, of witness and denial, of brokenness and healing, of trauma and peace. It is certainly a road of passion today – both in the sense that people experience great suffering and intense human emotions.

In this session notice how prayer and pain blend, how hopes and fears meet, as you feel the pulse and heartbeat of the living city. Listen to these voices of passion and hope – sometimes shocking or disturbing, sometimes revealing extraordinary courage and faith – reflecting the contemporary context for an ancient devotion.

Jesus walks this road not as one solitary individual from Nazareth, but as the new Adam, as everyman/everywoman, a corporate universal figure who gathers into himself the pain of the ages. As Suffering Servant, as we noted, he gathered unto himself the hopes and griefs of all people: "Surely he has borne our infirmities and carried our diseases (Isa 53:4). As Son of Man, he bears the pain of humanity. Matthew 25 invites us to look today for the features of Christ in the faces of those who suffer, to be alert to his presence in those who are hurting.

Even in the New Testament we get the sense that Jesus is suffering still, after his Resurrection. To Saul, the Risen Christ says: "I am Jesus and you are persecuting me" (Acts 9:4). The writer of Colossians speaks of his sufferings: "in my flesh I complete what is lacking in Christ's afflictions for the sake of his body, that is, his church" (Col 1:12). The Letter to the Hebrews suggests that it is possible to crucify Christ afresh (Heb 6:6). Pascal wrote: "Christ is in agony until the end of time." In our very midst he suffers and rises today. Today he falls down into the dirt and dust in the experience of those whose human rights are trampled upon.

This has particular resonance in the Holy Land. As Naim Ateek puts it in his *Contemporary Way of the Cross*: "For Palestinian Christians, the experience of Golgotha is not a distant past or sad memory; it is part of everyday indignity and oppression. Our Via Dolorosa is not a mere ritualistic procession through the narrow streets of the old city of Jerusalem but the fate of being subjugated and humiliated in our own land."

It is significant that the Via Dolorosa winds its way through the very center of the Old City of Jerusalem today. It begins at the northern edge of the Temple Mount, with all its Jewish associations and memories and at the selfsame moment it begins in the Muslim quarter with its present sadnesses. At points it is crossed by Jewish Orthodox hurrying down to prayer at the Western Wall, and at the same time it witnesses Muslim men kneeling on their mats at the time of prayer in their shops. It passes a place for the rehabilitation of blind refugees. Along its route today are found soldiers, beggars, pilgrims and tourists, street-sellers, laughing children and crippled elderly. This river of prayer and passion flows in the broken heart of the city, as a potential source of healing and forgiveness. As of old human characters were caught up into its drama and flow – Mary, Simon of Cyrene, Veronica, the weeping women – so today the Way of the Cross gathers into itself the joys and pains of the residents of the city who are going about their daily round. As we meet them here in the interviews you will read, we learn something new about living with courage in the face of trial.

Thus we can walk this Way and pray this Way in recognition of human trauma today. In prayer we seek the gift of empathy that we may glimpse, however faintly, how the Way of the Cross is a present reality across the world. Thus the Way of the Cross can become for us not only an act of intercession for all who find themselves treading a path of pain today, wherever in the world, but also an act of solidarity with all Christ's wounded and rising brothers and sisters.

CLOWNING & HURTING:
CHILDREN OF THE VIA DOLOROSA

Station 1 recalls where Jesus is judged by Pilate. Today, arising from the massive rock which once served as the foundation for Pontius Pilate's Antonia Fortress, myriad children's voices fill the air: where the Roman citadel built by Herod the Great once overlooked the Temple Mount, the Omariyya Boys' School stands proudly. Mohammed the school gate-keeper tells me that today nine hundred and fifty children study here, from the age of six to twelve years. Half come from the Old City itself, and half from Arab villages neighboring Jerusalem. The Arab population is young – the Central Board of Statistics reports that 42 percent of the Arab population is below the age of fifteen. Their cheerful voices betray hidden traumas. 75 percent of Arab children in Jerusalem live below the poverty line (as do 45 percent of Jewish children). They live in desperately overcrowded apartments, where the child is exposed to the adult world at an early point, and domestic violence is sometimes an expression of simmering frustration and anger at intolerable and unending stress in the city. Many have been traumatized by seeing first hand acts of political violence. The unremitting tensions in the Old City, which occasionally peak into street-violence, take their toll on the children as they grow up. Jantien, when Director of the nearby Spafford Children's Center, told me:

> There is a desperate shortage of school places for children. There are five thousand children of school age out of school in the Old City and East Jerusalem. At night, the children live on the street. By day the Via Dolorosa is crowded with pilgrims, but in the evening it is transformed: it becomes a playground, football pitch and cycle track! But one thing I have noticed about the children is how violent their play can be – pushing, screaming, cursing each other – kicking is the favorite of way of expressing yourself. Their play can be aggressive and spiteful. They bully each other sometimes. Guns are a favorite toy, even for the girls.
>
> There seems to be a cycle of violence. Children pick up stress from their parents who may be unemployed or desperately poor. Their flats will be impossibly crowded: maybe ten to a room. And there is a spiral of fear. Parents are well aware of the stresses of living under military occupation, and they pass this onto the children.
>
> The tribal society of the old city does have advantages. There is none of the isolation or loneliness children can feel in the West, where each home is behind its fence. Here it is life together, a close community, children in and out of each other's homes. We must not forget the childhood joys. Families are loving, and we hear children laughing and joking – they are not aware that they live under occupation. For them it is normal.

Station 2 marks where Jesus receives his cross. The Sisters of Our Lady of Zion came here in 1856, establishing a convent and school above a substantial stretch of Roman flagstones, identified for many years as the Gabbatha pavement or *lithostrotos* where Pilate gave judgment (John 19:13). The Ecce Homo arch which spans the street here traditionally marks the place where Pilate offered Jesus back to the crowd with the words: "Behold the man!" (John 19:5).

Led by their founder Fr Theodore Ratisbonne, the first mission of the sisters was to convert Jews. But everything changed during the Second World War. The sisters found themselves in Germany hiding and protecting Jewish children as the Holocaust unfolded. They asked: "How can such things happen in Christian Europe?" The Second Vatican Council's 1965 document *Nostra Aetate* ("The Relation of the Church to Non-Christian Religions") opened up new perspectives for inter-religious dialogue, and today the Sisters help facilitate face-to-face meetings between Christians and Jews and teach Biblical studies with a focus on Jewish sources.

On the street one hears the shrieks of children playing in the school-yard, the robust hymn-singing of Spanish pilgrims, and the air-piercing cry of the muezzin-call to prayer from the minaret; on a Friday at dusk the Jew-ish siren announcing the arrival of the Sabbath completes the cacophony. Here the traditions face each other. One Sister tells me:

> We are all children of God – and children of Abraham! We want to create safe places where genuine encounter can take place. Since the uprisings dialogue has been more difficult – the trust level has deteriorated and the hatred has grown. Fear holds people back. We are teaching Hebrew to our Arabic staff here, because the alterna-tive to demonizing the Other is learning the language of the Other. We have to see the Other as a human being and as a child of God. It would be easy to give up on all this, but we hold on – we have to live the Christian value of hope. We have to stand beside people with hope.

Another Sister speaks of the pain of this street:

> Today the Via Dolorosa is still a way of tears. Here, at the second station Jesus received his cross – and I feel that he still receives it today in the people of the Palestinians, Christian and Muslim. There is a constant cry for help here, and despair all around. They feel that the world is not concerned. They feel unwanted and de-spised. Jesus continues to suffer in these children. The Via Dolo-rosa is not just a historical event but a daily reality, and not only on this street but at the checkpoints, where there is daily humiliation and degradation for children just trying to get to school or folk to work. Some of our staff have to queue up each day for two hours and they are treated like animals at the checkpoints. Even here, on this street, sometimes the city gate is closed and we can't get food supplies in for the guesthouse, or building supplies. The frustra-tion level is sometimes very high. There are daily complications with soldiers everywhere and restrictions imposed all the time. But is still a privilege to live here, so close to where Jesus walked.
>
> Our role is to walk alongside others on this way of sorrows. Palestinians have a heavy cross to bear and we walk with them. But living in the Muslim Quarter and also working with the Jewish people, makes us open to both. We do not take sides – there have been mistakes on both sides. We can love and respect the Jewish people, even if we do not approve of Israeli policies. And we have

to remember: even though Jesus was a Man of Sorrows, he was not a miserable, unhappy person! We remember Christ's suffering and death but we do continue to live and enjoy life! That is the paradox. Our faith is grounded in suffering. We turn to God and have a greater trust in God when there is difficulty and suffering. God is compassionate. And this road: perhaps more prayers are offered here than any place!

FALLING & STANDING: YOUTH ON THE VIA DOLOROSA

Station 3 recalling where Jesus collapses the first time under the weight of the Cross and through the fatigue of his torture is marked by a Polish chapel at the junction where the Via Dolorosa meets El Wad Street. He crashes to the ground and lies in the dust, before pulling himself up once again and standing erect. This theme resonates strongly in the stories of the young people who find themselves here today.

The Jewish people were crushed to the earth in the experience of the Holocaust, but now they find themselves standing upright and defiant. This is represented strongly in the soldiers of the Israeli Defense Force. Dressed in green combat uniform, two teenage Israeli soldiers stand up defiant and in control, their automatic rifles slung over their shoulders, finger ever on the trigger. Their presence on the Via Dolorosa reminds us of the military forces Jesus faced: soldiers, based in their barracks in the Antonia Fortress, escorted him along the street (Mark 15:22) and the commander or centurion stood by the cross (Mark 15:39). Today's soldiers, stationed on the corner right outside the third station church, maintain a military presence on the busiest stretch of the Via Dolorosa, where Jews rush down to pray at the Western Wall, Muslims to pray at the Al Aqsa Mosque, and Christians follow the way of the cross. Shmuel (19), rifle now in hand, explains:

> This is a problem area. We're here to guard Jewish homes in the Muslim quarter. We also keep a look out as Jewish people go down to the Wall. We don't want them attacked. We have to make sure they're safe as they go to pray. You never know what to expect from the terrorists. We have to look out for anything – even Molotov cocktails [petrol bombs]. You can feel the tension sometimes. It's not good here, it's not fun, anything could happen! We're proud to be here, because we are protecting the Jewish people. We're proud to serve our country. No more questions!

Close by, a balcony extends over the narrow Via Dolorosa, with three large Israeli flags, the Star of David, blowing defiantly in the breeze. The building is identified by a sign which says: "Igud Lohamay: the Association of the Fighters of the Battle for Jerusalem." A seminary or yeshiva had been founded here by a Polish rabbi in 1886. The occupants fled from the building during the 1936 Arab riots, but before they left they put a trusted Arab family in charge, who walled up the entrance to the synagogue/ study room on the first floor. It was to remain hidden from view until June 1967, when Israeli soldiers, taking charge of the Old City, regained possession of this building. With great joy they unwalled the synagogue, its contents untouched for thirty one years. Today it is a thriving traditional yeshiva. Hanuch, a student in his twenties explains:

> We need to be here. It's our land, our city. Since '67, we are back! We don't like this being called the "Muslim Quarter" – for us, it is the renewed Jewish Quarter, because Jews have been living on this street since the nineteenth century. We are witnessing the Redemption of the Land. We are getting ready for the coming of the Messiah. Today we have two hundred students here, from all over Israel, to study the Torah, to get ready.
>
> We feel safe in the building because we have security guards. But we are not allowed to walk down the street to the Kotel [Western Wall] by ourselves in the evening. We need two armed guards, with their guns ready, to accompany us past the Arab homes and shops. It's just too dangerous for us. The Rabbi forbids us going alone. By day the Arabs concentrate on stealing from the tourists. At night they concentrate on us. They will spit at us, or worse! So we have worry living here. But it's the greatest privilege to be close to where the Temple was, and where one day it will be rebuilt!

Station 7 recalling where Jesus stumbles and falls the second time is marked by a chapel at the junction of the Via Dolorosa and the busy Khan ez Zeit – which runs the route of the ancient Roman cardo. Alae, who works for the Old City Counselling Center for young people, talks about how Palestinian young people are falling repeatedly today in the city.

> The Center's been here for eleven years. It is supported by the Latin Patriarchate. Right now we are helping sixty young people from the Old City and East Jerusalem on drugs, mainly in their twenties. Forty per cent of them are injecting heroin. About a quarter are Christians – the rest are Muslims.

They have got trapped in a circle. They are under such pressures. There are no jobs for them, few chances to study, overcrowded homes, no sports facilities on the Arab side of the city. And the Wall [Separation Barrier] cuts them off from their wider families. They feel alone. They take drugs to escape all this, then they get into debt, stealing to support the habit, going into petty crime. Then sometimes they get put in jails or detention centers but often the Israeli police don't seem to bother with them. The soldiers and police are more preoccupied with security issues, watching over the house evictions and demolitions in Silwan. In the West Bank our police really clamp down on the drugs. But here?

Really the young people are swinging between two worlds: going to the new city, with its discos and parties, and belonging to very traditional families in the Old City, where young people are expected to stay in. Really Arab society here is tribal and individual achievement is not always encouraged. It is not like the individualism of the West with its competition between people.

But there are some young people, of course, who want to aim higher, they have creative ideas and want to make something of themselves. At our Center we lead a program for youth empowerment – leadership training. We teach creative thinking – getting them to see what they can do, creative things, art things, in the schools and hospitals, designing things. We try to give them their confidence back. They can be useful – they can do good! They might be pushed down, but they can get up again!

REACHING OUT:
WOMEN ON THE VIA DOLOROSA

On the Via Dolorosa there are three poignant meetings between Jesus and women. Jesus comes face to face with his mother, as she powerlessly looks on at the agony and distress of her son, a son she once cradled at Bethlehem and nurtured in Nazareth. Later Jesus meets a woman to whom tradition has assigned the name "Veronica" – meaning "true image." As she steps forward to wipe the bloodied face of Jesus, the imprint of his features is left upon the cloth. Soon afterwards, Jesus encounters a group of women in deepest grief, bewailing him loudly. We meet the women of Jerusalem who live in these sacred spots today.

Station 4 is marked by an Armenian Catholic Church built in 1905, its altar crowned by an octagonal cupola so distinctive of Armenian architecture. In the courtyard outside the Church stands a memorial to the Armenian holocaust: the memory of the suffering lies deep within the Armenian collective consciousness. On the street, Aneesa, who is in her forties, sits in the gutter where Jesus met his Mother. She is perched on an upturned plastic crate, meters away from the young Israeli soldiers on duty at the corner where the Via Dolorosa meets the busy El Wad Street (valley street). She wears the traditional Palestinian ankle-length dress, black with stunning embroidery in different colors on the chest, while a white scarf covers her hair. She is surrounded by clusters of vegetables and sells sprigs of basil, parsley, thyme for two shekels a piece, making 30 shekels day for her family in Bethlehem. She is always reaching out her hand to passersby. Sitting in the dust of the gutter, she somehow maintains a quiet dignity in the midst of it all. She seems resigned to her fate, but is grateful for everything, for little things. She peppers every sentence with *hamdulillah* - "thanks be to God!"

> I have five children, three girls and two boys, thanks be to God. They are aged between two and twelve – the twelve year old really looks after the family, as my husband is very sick. He is fifty. He can't work, he has big heart problems - he has often in the hospital, and the fees are so high, I can hardly pay them. I get home to see the children once in two weeks. I have to sleep rough in the Old City every night, wherever I can find a space! I often get cold but, thanks be to God, I have my jumper. In Bethlehem we all live in one room. That is all we have. No telephone, and I don't have a mobile, to stay in touch with the family. We have electricity – thanks be to God – and we have a well for water.
>
> I could be arrested here, as I am from the West Bank and don't have all the papers and permits to sell things. Somehow I get through the Wall. Here the soldiers leave me alone. They are interested in the young men, always stopping them and asking them for their ID.
>
> I have never stopped to think if things could be any different. We say *enshallah* for everything – "if God wills . . . " I expect nothing. We just survive, week to week. I have no options to do anything else. What else can I do? I don't have hope of any change. But we do survive: thanks be to God. I go to the Al Aqsa mosque– that is special. God looks after us. Now you make me smile. You are the first person to take notice of me and speak to me in weeks!

Station 6 is celebrated by a Greek Catholic Church dedicated to the memory of St Veronica and cared for since 1948 by Charles de Foucauld's order of Little Sisters of Jesus. Sister Rose, a German, has lived here since 1997 and is part of a community today of five sisters here. The story of the sixth station tells how Veronica, stepping out of the crowd, comes forward to wipe the face of Jesus as he passes carrying his cross. The imprint of his features is left indelibly on the cloth. How does the community identify with Veronica's experience?

> We aim to live a contemplative life in the midst of the city, to be with God and to be with the people. Like Jesus in Nazareth we work with our hands, we live a simple, poor life. We try to wipe the face of Jesus today, as we see his face in the poor, in the pilgrims, the Muslim residents of this street, in all people. What is very, very important is building up relationships, bit by bit, with all our neighbors. We share in their good moments and bad, in their births, marriages and deaths. Our motto is: *Notre vocation est être*. Our vocation is being, being here, with Jesus, with the people. Jesus is here, he is with the people. And we are just living in the midst of it all, a tiny witness to Christ's love.

Station 8, marked by a Cross in the wall, commemorates the moment Jesus speaks to the women of Jerusalem. Here Steph, a young German evangelical woman, runs St John's Hospice, a fourteen bed guesthouse, with her husband. They are members of the lay evangelical community of Christus-Teff, based near Frankfurt, and live here alongside young volunteers as part of a community of five. Steph shares:

> I reflect on what it means to me to live so close to the spot where Jesus speaks to the women of Jerusalem: "weep for yourselves". This has a vital message for us today. Jesus is honoring women. Today – the Jewish women are stuck in the home, the Muslim women are oppressed by conventions. Jesus speaks to the women of Jerusalem and he empowers them, he tells them to take responsibility for themselves: "Don't weep for me..." He says, don't worry about me, think of yourselves, what you can do. You can change the world bit by bit!

Up the street Hela heads the Melia Art and Training Center on behalf of the Arab Orthodox Society for the Relief of the Sick. Established in 1990, it empowers and trains women in needlework skills on the West Bank and here in its shop sells the stunning embroidery – dresses, bags and stoles – made by the Palestinian women, raising vital cash for families living in poverty. Hela is an active member of the St James' Arab Orthodox Church:

their parish church is the ancient building adjoining the Holy Sepulcher's great belfry, a stone's throw from Calvary. Hela testifies:

> Jesus understands the pain of this street. His sufferings, his sacrifice . . . he understands. I ask Jesus to carry what I am carrying, the worry and the stress. This makes me feel more free. He helps me. He says to me: "As I carry the cross for you, bear your burdens patiently. I will carry then with you." So I say to him: "This worry is yours, it's not mine!"
>
> My heart opened to God when I joined with other Christians to pray for justice and for Christian unity in this city. Before, I did follow religion, but it was cold and dutiful. My faith came alive when I joined the ecumenical prayer group – we meet each Tuesday afternoon to encourage each other and to pray for the city. Now I see the Resurrection in everything, even in little things – especially in little things: the flower opening on my terrace, the bird dancing in the sunlight. These are precious gifts of God. These are signs of spiritual life. You see the Resurrection every day in your life, and in the strength you get. Jesus gives us love to share with the Muslims, and with those difficult to love. We have to care for our neighbors and for the weak. His rising is everyday. Look for it!

BEARING BURDENS:
MEN ON THE VIA DOLOROSA

Station 5, recalling how Simon of Cyrene helps Jesus carry his cross, is marked by a small chapel on the corner of El Wad street. At this very point today in the street, we encounter a range of men, each in his own way carrying a heavy burden, some feeling they are outsiders in this city: all are sons or fathers with anxieties for their future. Some, like Jesus, feel crushed into the ground by the cross they have to bear.

Tucked away behind the façades of shops which line the Via Dolorosa near the fifth station are found very different workshops. David (50) has a small house adjoining both the station's chapel and a synagogue owned by the Institute of Talmudic Studies, established in a building taken over in 1999. David had stones thrown at his children playing in the courtyard below when the Old City Settlers first moved in above the synagogue. He runs a small workshop here and is an accomplished craftsman in olive wood, fashioning figures of Jesus carrying his cross for pilgrims.

I love this wood. The olive tree is very special to us Palestinians. Its roots go deep down into the soil, like us. It belongs to the land. It is us and our future. The trees give us oil, for soap and cooking and medicine, and wood for this carving. It makes me so angry when I hear that settlers cut down thousands of our trees this year, and the Wall has destroyed so many. This wood – look at it – the clear parts and the parts with such lovely grain. When the wood is green it can be cut quickly by machine, but I work with the dry wood and do it all by hand. I choose each piece carefully. It takes me three days to make each piece. I cannot sell it for ten shekels! It is my life! We cut the wood carefully so it doesn't hurt the tree. We may take off a branch but you know, the olive tree never dies. It will grow again another branch. Like us!

The pilgrims on the street don't often stop to buy anything from my shop here. They keep their heads down in their prayer-books and beads – they are so caught up in their prayers they don't seem even to notice us. They don't stop to speak to us! Christians need to open their eyes!

Station 9, where Jesus falls the third time, is marked by an ancient pillar outside the Coptic Church of St Helena. Here sits Fr Mikael, a Coptic priest of 43 years. He has lived here for eleven years.

Fourteen monks live here. We welcome pilgrims every day to the Coptic Church and this great cistern which Helena built. Some-times I miss the great silence of my monastery of Anba Bishoi in the Wadi Natrun of Egypt. It goes back to the fourth century, it is a monastery of the desert fathers. Here is it very noisy. Sometimes settlers in the city spit at us and abuse us. They are against us. We are pushed down all the time, like Jesus at the ninth station. We are pushed down, down, down.

DYING & RISING:
PASTORS ON THE VIA DOLOROSA

Station 10, remembering how Jesus is stripped prior to his crucifixion, is to be found in the awesome basilica of the Holy Sepulcher, in the Latin chapel beside Calvary. It can be reached by crossing the Ethiopian monastery, an African village in the heart of Jerusalem. On the roof of St Helena's Chapel – that part of the Holy Sepulcher exposing the deep quarry where Constan-tine's mother found the true Cross – lives a community of five Ethiopian monks. Their little monastic cells have been built of mud bricks amidst the ruins of the medieval Crusader cloister, but the Ethiopian Christian presence in Jerusalem goes back to at least the fourth century. Gerama, in his seventies, has lived nearby since 1968, helps look after the property and is involved in the pastoral care of the community. He speaks of the two proudest Ethiopian traditions linked to the Bible. Looking up to the sky, raising his arms in a gesture towards heaven, Gerama exclaims:

> This is the Monastery of the King, we call it "Deir es Sultan." The Bible tells you about the visit of our Queen, the Queen of Sheba, to King Solomon, son of David. Solomon fathered with her the first emperor of Ethiopia, Menelik. And the Acts of the Apostles tells you about the conversion of the first Ethiopian by St Philip as he traveled the road from Jerusalem to Gaza. He is the first Ethiopian Christian. So we have been coming here ever since!
>
> We have only five sisters here now up the street in the convent and they are very old. And we have five brothers living here on the roof. They rise for prayers at four every morning. They cook for themselves very simple stuff, they are very poor. I see tears in their eyes very often . . . My joy? I have one joy, despite it all. Living here is the gift of God!

Station 11 commemorating the nailing of Jesus and Station 12, the death of Jesus, are marked by chapels built atop the rocky limestone outcrop of Calvary and nearby the tomb of Jesus recalls Stations 13 and 14, the taking down from the Cross and the burial. A stone's throw away stands the Lutheran Church of the Redeemer where Ibrahim Azar has been pastor to a congregation of four hundred, drawn from members from ninety families – in 2017 he was elected bishop for the Evangelical Lutheran Church in Jordan and the Holy Land. Its four schools educate Christians and Muslim students side by side and have a strong ethos of teaching tolerance and peacebuilding.

> We all identify with Jesus in the Cross. He identifies with us. We sometimes feel so isolated and vulnerable. What we have to remember is this: God didn't stay on the Cross. He didn't stay in the tomb. He went out and gave life to the people. We live now between Easter and the Great Resurrection at the end. We have to place our present troubles in this big perspective, and not let them cloud our hope. We are people of faith. We live in the faith of the Resurrection!

QUESTIONS

Reflecting on your encounters with each group, consider these questions and look up the pertinent Scriptures:

1. What do the people of this road reveal to us about living with courage everyday?

2. What does this say to you in your situation?

3. What lines in the interviews strike you? Why?

4. What are the sorrows and hopes of this age range or group in your own neighborhood? How can you and friends respond to them?

> **Children:** Read Mark 9:31–37 and 10:13–16 (child in the midst).
>
> **Young men:** Read I John 1:12–17 (address to young men).
>
> **Women:** Read Luke 23:27–31 (Jesus speaks to the women).
>
> **Men:** Read 2 Timothy 1:3–7 (Paul's advice to Timothy)
>
> **Pastors:** Read Romans 6:1- 14 (Easter hope).

PRAYER EXERCISE

Today's Way of the Cross

The petitions are grouped in threes, and one phrase of "Lord have mercy, Christ have mercy, Lord have mercy" may be said after each. At each station, the first two petitions relate to Jerusalem today, and the third relates to our own home situation. This is reprinted, with material above, from Mayes, *Gateways to the Divine: Transformative Pathways of Prayer from the Holy City of Jerusalem.*

I Jesus is condemned to death

Jesus, you are judged before Pilate: give the little ones of this place a carefree childhood, free from the oppressive judgment or control of others.

Jesus, you are crowned with thorns: heal the trauma of all children damaged by the violence of others.

Jesus, scourged and beaten, enable us to draw close to those who are bruised in our own communities.

II Jesus receives his cross

Jesus, the cross is laid upon your shoulders: give to parents wisdom and patience as they accept the weight of their responsibilities in an uncertain world.

Jesus, you begin your journey: bless the Sisters of Zion and inspire all the Children of Abraham – Jew, Muslim and Christian – to walk the risky journey of mutual understanding and trust.

Jesus, Man of Sorrows and Man of Joy, help us to restore laughter to children who are robbed of childhood innocence.

III Jesus falls first time

Jesus, you are crushed with the weight of the cross: give to Shmuel and all soldiers compassion and humanity in their dealings with others.

Jesus, you find yourself in the dust of the street, give to Hanuch and to all the students of the Jewish yeshiva the grace to study your Law in humility and tolerance.

Jesus, you are brought low: lead us from sympathy to empathy, and give us the grace to get right alongside the brokenhearted and downcast.

IV Jesus meets his mother

Jesus, you receive Mary's touch: comfort all parents anxious for the fate of the children.

Jesus, you are sustained by Mary's look into your eyes: restore dignity to Aneesa and all who find themselves in the gutter of the street.

Jesus, your heart goes out to your own mother: give us the wisdom to speak words of encouragement to all mothers who are stressed or depressed.

V Simon of Cyrene helps carry the cross

Jesus, you need Simon's help in bearing the cross: sustain David and the men of the city who carry heavy weights of fear, insecurity and worry for their families.

Jesus, you share our infirmities: cheer and hearten those who reveal your care to others.

Jesus, you accepted the support of another: help us to step out from the crowd to relive the burdens of those hurting in our community.

VI Veronica wipes the face of Jesus

Jesus, you accept Veronica's gesture of comfort: bless the Little Sisters of Jesus as they extend Veronica's loving touch today.

Jesus, you reveal your face to Veronica: help us to discern your features in the lives of those who suffer.

Jesus, you give an imprint to Veronica's cloth: impress on our hearts the image of your love.

VII Jesus falls the second time

Jesus, you are crushed by the weight of the cross: lighten the hearts of all young people burdened by frustration and loss of opportunity.

Jesus, you find yourself brought low once again: raise up to a new future young people pulled down by drug abuse and loss of self-worth.

Jesus, falling down and rising again, give us courage, vision and perseverance in developing our ministry to young people where we live.

VIII Jesus meets the women of Jerusalem

Jesus, you greet the women of the city: hearten and empower Jewish, Muslim and Christian women, who seek to take new responsibility for their futures, as we remember Aneesa, Sister Rose, Steph and Hela.

Jesus, you look upon the tears of the women: strengthen all women who are degraded, exploited or oppressed.

Jesus, you honored the potential of the women of Jerusalem: show us how to welcome and respect the dignity and gifting of women in our churches today.

IX Jesus falls the third time

Jesus, you stumble again to the ground: sustain and uplift the most fragile and vulnerable Christians of Jerusalem, remembering Gerama and Fr Mikael.

Jesus, your body is fatigued and broken: heal the wounds in your body the church.

Jesus, torn and bruised of body, help us to work for the unity of your people in our locality.

X Jesus is stripped

Jesus, you are stripped of your clothes: restore the dignity of all who feel denuded and exposed to danger.

Jesus, you are exposed to abuse: we pray for those who hurl insults at one another in this city today.

Jesus, bearing our shame, strip us of all judgmental attitudes and hardness of heart.

XI Jesus is nailed to the Cross

Jesus, you open wide your arms to embrace the world: encompass with your love all who are seeking the Divine today across the globe.

Jesus, your body is pieced with five wounds: draw close to those wounded by violent actions in the city of Jerusalem.

Jesus . . . ..help us to leave at the cross our failures, our fears, and our frustrations.

XII Jesus dies on the cross

Jesus, dying on the cross, help Ibrahim and all pastors to reflect your undying love to others.

Jesus, you share utterly and completely the pains of humanity: enfold and embrace those who suffer in the Holy Land today.

Jesus, breathing your last, help us to exhale from our hearts every judgmental attitude towards others.

XIII The body of Jesus is taken down from the Cross

Jesus, laid in the arms of your mother, comfort all who grieve for losses or bereavements of any kind.

Jesus, your life looks finished and over: draw close to those trapped in despondency or fatalism.

Jesus, you are the new Adam opening up a new future for the world, fill with unshakable hope all who work for peace and reconciliation.

XIV The body of Jesus is laid in the tomb

Jesus, your body is safely placed in the tomb: bless all who care for and protect the holy places today.

Jesus, awaiting resurrection, be close to all Jews Christians and Muslims who find themselves watching and waiting for a better world.

Jesus, in the deepest darkness you kindle the light of new life, ignite and enflame in us the faith of Easter, that with the Christians of Jerusalem we may witness to your Gospel by lives radiant and incandescent with hope, Amen!

> **Almighty God,**
> **whose most dear Son went not up to joy but first he suffered pain,**
> **and entered not into glory before he was crucified:**
> **mercifully grant that we, walking in the way of the cross,**
> **may find it none other than the way of life and peace;**
> **through Jesus Christ your Son our Lord.**

Helping one another on Roman Road near Moza

5

The Road to Emmaus
Building Unbreakable Hope

THE ROAD TO EMMAUS is a place of surprising encounter, yesterday and today. Cleopas and his companion, as they walked this way downcast and depressed, found their hearts burning within them as they discovered the Risen Christ:

> Now on that same day two of them were going to a village called Emmaus, about seven miles from Jerusalem, and talking with each other about all these things that had happened. While they were talking and discussing, Jesus himself came near and went with them, but their eyes were kept from recognizing him. And he said to them, "What are you discussing with each other while you walk along?" They stood still, looking sad. Then one of them, whose name was Cleopas, answered him, "Are you the only stranger in Jerusalem who does not know the things that have taken place there in these days?" He asked them, "What things?" They replied, "The things about Jesus of Nazareth, who was a prophet mighty in deed and word before God and all the people, and how our chief priests and leaders handed him over to be condemned to death and crucified him. But we had hoped that he was the one to redeem Israel. . . . " Then he said to them, "Oh, how foolish you are, and how slow of heart to believe all that the prophets have declared! Was it not necessary that the Messiah should suffer these things and then enter into his glory?" Then beginning with Moses

and all the prophets, he interpreted to them the things about himself in all the scriptures.

As they came near the village to which they were going, he walked ahead as if he were going on. But they urged him strongly, saying, "Stay with us, because it is almost evening and the day is now nearly over." So he went in to stay with them. When he was at the table with them, he took bread, blessed and broke it, and gave it to them. Then their eyes were opened, and they recognized him; and he vanished from their sight. They said to each other, "Were not our hearts burning within us while he was talking to us on the road, while he was opening the scriptures to us?" That same hour they got up and returned to Jerusalem; and they found the eleven and their companions gathered together. They were saying, "The Lord has risen indeed, and he has appeared to Simon!" Then they told what had happened on the road, and how he had been made known to them in the breaking of the bread. (Luke 24: 13–35)

Several possible locations have been identified for the site of Emmaus. The first we will visit is, indeed, a Roman road on which it is possible still to walk.

MOZA: THE ROMAN ROAD

From the direction of Jerusalem, an evocative Roman road in the pineclad Sorek valley leads to Moza, which scholars now favor as the most likely location for the Luke's story (see Thiede's book *The Emmaus Mystery*). It was perhaps along this road that David danced his way to Jerusalem from Kiriath-Jearim in front of the Ark of the Covenant according to 2 Samuel 6. The site of Moza is called Ammaous by Josephus in his *Jewish War*, and later it becomes known as Colonia after the Roman army veterans established a colony there. Archaeologists have located Herodian structures, bespeaking a leafy suburb of Jerusalem, and Byzantine and Crusader remains. Nearby, lies today's "road into the future" – the highway which modern travelers must take on their way from the holy city to the airport at the conclusion of a pilgrimage: there is the juxtaposition of the noisy motorway with its traffic roaring through the narrow gorge and the silence of the adjoining valley served by the ancient road. Indeed, the modern highway, follows an ancient trade route between Jerusalem and the Mediterranean ports.

As pilgrims walk on remnants of Roman pavements near Moza, in a gorge cut into 300 foot limestone cliffs, the road itself becomes a parable about encountering the Risen Christ. Four things strike the pilgrim-walker.

First, this road to Emmaus is a risky place to walk. The valley is exposed, and the road is eroded and hazardous. Its surface is uneven, and one can stumble up over broken stones. The place where the Risen Christ waits to meet the traveler is not the place of a comfortable stroll, but the place of risk and vulnerability. Sometimes the deep peace of this road is shattered by unnerving volleys from a nearby firing range, where young soldiers are trained in target practice, the sound ricocheting in the tranquil valley. Sometimes helicopters swoop deafeningly overhead. Yes, the road to Emmaus feels here risky.

Secondly, the walker needs to have a wakeful alertness, and literally watch one's step. But like Cleopas one should not be looking down all the time, eyes to the ground. Not only would the walker miss the natural beauty of the gorge, with its fragrant conifers, but one might also miss the presence of an Other, the Stranger who draws close. This is a call to walk the road as contemplatives in movement: to contemplate is literally to "look attentively": Cleopas was given the gift of eyes that were opened (Luke 24:31).

A third lesson to be learned from the road to Emmaus, as it is experienced near Moza, concerns Christian community. Here pilgrims must help one another on the road – giving each other a hand, especially where there is the need to climb up onto the Roman curb, or step over an obstacle in the path.

Finally, the road needs these days to be cleared as one walks – the pathway is strewn with fallen branches and rocks, over which one might trip. We need to clear a pathway, and remove from it the detritus and the occasional garbage. The path needs to be decluttered: as one walks, one must remove impediments in order to progress in the journey. There are many things to be learnt in the Holy Land from the roads, which speak to our ongoing spiritual journey. A contrast may be drawn between tourists and pilgrims: the word "tourist" coming from the Old French word for "tower" suggests that the traveler sees things from a safe, uninvolved distance; the word pilgrim derives from the Latin *per agri*, meaning "beyond the fields," suggesting the image of one who is prepared to take a risky road, less known. What will we be?

NICOPOLIS: COMMUNITY OF THE BEATITUDES

At one of the possible sites of Emmaus – Nicopolis – the catholic, contemplative and charismatic Community of the Beatitudes has lived since 1993. Here have been located stunning remains of the Byzantine church built in the fifth century to celebrate the story of the road to Emmaus. In 1877 the Carmelite community of Bethlehem acquired the site and in the 1930s the Fathers of Betharram built a convent. Fr Franz, the Prior, explains:

> We are a community of eleven: three brothers, four sisters, two lay people and two enquirers, comprising eight different nationalities. That is a miracle of the resurrection in itself: Christ bringing together such different people to be his Body in this place. We see our vocation as working for mutual understanding and reconciliation between Christians and Jews. The story of Emmaus is about two people walking side by side on a journey, with the Risen Christ drawing alongside. We seek to walk with the Jewish people, and build bridges to Judaism. There is a lot of misunderstanding. Christians still border on anti-Semitism, while Jews often see Christianity as idolatrous. We have to conquer prejudices little by little and the way to do this is the way of encounter, of meeting, of sharing across the traditions. The good thing is that people are curious: Israelis are curious, for example, about what Christians really believe. So we host a monthly meeting here for Jews and Christians, rabbis and religious and others come together as we explore common themes like creation, Noah, covenant, forgiveness . . . .We also visit synagogues and host what we call spiritual concerts, where we can appreciate the different traditions through music. On Friday nights we welcome the arrival of the Sabbath. On Saturdays we have a charismatic vigil of prayer followed by Israeli dances to celebrate the resurrection! On Sundays we go to Tel Aviv to lead teaching sessions. The Emmaus story is marked by questions: the questions of the travelers, and the questions of the Risen Christ.
>
> At the heart of our ministry is the Eucharist. Jesus revealed himself in the breaking of the bread. So we have perpetual exposition of the Blessed Sacrament and there is always one member of the community praying before the Sacrament through the day in adoration or intercession.
>
> Because we are located just off the highway between the airport and Jerusalem, this holy place is often where groups may begin or end their pilgrimages. The message of this place is be

alert to the presence of the Risen Christ, wherever he may like to surprise you!

QUBEIBEH: FRANCISCAN COMMUNITY

There is another site for Emmaus: the liturgical Emmaus at Qubeibeh, on the occupied West Bank, where hundreds of Christian pilgrims come for the Franciscans' Easter Monday Eucharist, each worshipper given a small loaf of bread to take home. Its Roman street and ancient Jewish houses form an evocative scene, where we can imagine Cleopas and his companion walking side-by-side with the Risen Christ. But normally, today, this road to Emmaus is blocked. Only courageous pilgrims will attempt this path, with the delay and humiliation of its military checkpoints. While the site is seven miles from Jerusalem, as in Luke's account (24:13), one must travel a circuitous route of twenty miles in order to reach it, due to road closures. This road to Emmaus goes through dark, unlit underpasses beneath the setters' bypass roads and in places it is hemmed in, to right and to left, by the towering walls of the Separation Barrier. But it is worth the trouble, as the topography holds more clues for our understanding. Where was Jesus bound, as he took this road? From this Emmaus you can taste the sea: beyond the ancient, terraced rocky hillsides lies the coastal plain, and from the church which marks the house of Cleopas and from the Roman road beside it, one can glimpse the port of Jaffa in the shimmering distance, and the Mediterranean itself. In the evening, you can feel the cooling sea breezes in your face.

The little community here consists of two Italian friars and three Franciscan sisters from the Philippines. It is a community that feels fragile and exposed, totally surrounded by a Muslim population: there are just four Christian families in the local town of perhaps 2000 Muslims. Sister Bonifacia tells me:

> Sometimes we feel very vulnerable. Sometimes the Muslim presence around us feels intimidating and threatening. Because of grinding poverty and economic gloom I think there are one or two rogues in the neighborhood, who steal and break into homes. In fact last month they cut into and sold to another person the internet connection of the little Salvadorian family nearby!
>
> St Francis told us that there are two ways in which we can live and witness among the Muslims. In the Earlier Rule, Francis talks about those who are to go among the Muslims (Saracens)

and unbelievers. First, he says, just be there: live in their midst, be a patient witness, don't look for results. Second, speak the Word of God when it is appropriate to God, when God directs. So we try to live this double way of presence and proclamation. As presence we exist to open up the holy place of Emmaus and its sanctuary to all who would come here. Once a year, on Easter Monday, we are able to welcome hundreds to the great Emmaus mass conducted by the Custos [Franciscan Custodian] of the Holy Land. But usually, we exist here as a quiet center of hospitality and welcome. And we open our gates daily to the local people. We have opened up a special space for the local Muslims. Next to the Church – in typical Franciscan fashion! – is a playground for the Muslim kids. There is a football pitch and swings for them to enjoy each day after school. So the holy domain of Emmaus is a church and a playground! All is holy – there is no division between finding the Risen Christ in the Church at the altar and finding him in the laughter and cries of the kids kicking a football around. And in a building built originally as a seminary, we have created a kindergarten where local Muslim mothers come each day with their preschool children. We don't make any charge for this, it is offered freely to the neighborhood. We ask nothing back in return. I work here, and try to get alongside them with the love of the Risen Christ.

All this is our ministry of presence. We just want to serve the community and promote good relations, healing relations. As for proclamation, it often is offered in these ways, wordlessly. For Francis said, "Preach the Gospel at all times, and use words if necessary!" By opening up our domain and sanctuary, we are preaching the love of God. And we proclaim it through the bell! The Muslims' mosque is right next to us here and they blast the deafening cry to prayer five times a day from their muezzin. It goes right through you! So we ring our church bell from the bell tower as often as we can! That is a form of proclamation. All this is how we live the resurrection.

ALWAYS GOING FURTHER

The elusive nature of Emmaus – we are not sure where exactly it was – has its own message. It might be your town! The risen Christ longs to greet us in the breaking of bread wherever we might live.

And what of those enigmatic words of Luke 24:28, translated in different ways?

> As they came near the village to which they were going, he walked ahead as if he were going on. (NRSV)
> As they approached the village to which they were going, Jesus continued on as if he were going farther. (KJV)
> About this time, they are nearing their destination. Jesus keeps walking ahead as if He has no plans to stop there . . . (*Voice*)

We gain the impression that Jesus doesn't want us to rest too much at some wayside inn. He doesn't want us to lapse into a complacency where we think we have arrived. Rather, he wants to lead us further along the road, and maybe into as yet unexplored roads; he beckons us into the future he opens before us. He wants us to risk new adventures.

In this course we have trodden five significant roads. We have walked in the footsteps of Abraham and Sarah through the central highlands, still troubled lands today.

We have taken the great trade route which has led us to pause at Gaza and Capernaum. We have descended into "the valley of the shadow of death" – that dangerous road by the ravine leading from Jerusalem to Jericho. We have walked with Jesus on the Way of the Cross, and found ourselves in company, not only with Mary, Veronica and Simon of old, but also with those who walk this pathway today.

But we have only just begun. Other roads and pathways summon us. The dying, rising Christ, who has trod with humanity paths of trial and hope, urges us to keep moving in our journey of faith. And as he shows at Emmaus, he is already on the road, ready to walk ahead of us into the future.

QUESTIONS

1. What is your experience of encountering the unexpected on your spiritual journey? Did this lead you to conversion or to change in any way?

2. In the book of Isaiah God says: "remove every obstruction from my people's way" (57:14) and "build up the highway, clear it of stones" (62:10). What impediments to your spiritual progress can you name: what roadblocks do you need to overcome if you are to continue to advance in the spiritual journey?

3. The presence of roadblocks in the occupied territories of the Holy Land raises questions about fundamental rights to freedom of travel and human dignity. How are people in your own context prevented or held back from achieving their true potential? What blocks people's movement towards discovering their self-worth and fulfilment?

4. "But we had hoped that he was the one to redeem Israel . . . " How do you respond when your hopes seem to be dashed? How can we open ourselves to fresh hope? (Notice in the account "their eyes were closed"; "their eyes were opened").

5. How do you find yourself responding to the prayer: " Lord Jesus, as this day begins, we remember that you are risen—therefore we look to the future with confidence"?

6. Read Romans 8:18–25. What is hope, for you? How can we build hope in and for one another?

PRAYER EXERCISE

Look again at the five questions that punctuate the conversation on the road in Luke 24. Notice how there are questions from Jesus to the disciples, questions from them to Jesus, and a question they address to themselves. So,

First, what questions to Jesus arise in your soul as this course closes?

Second, what is he asking of you?

Third, noting the last question in the Emmaus account, where the disciples ask themselves "Did not our hearts burn within us?", what are you asking of yourself at this point in time?

End by reflecting on the line "Then they told what had happened on the road, and how he had been made known to them . . . " What has happened to you on the five roads we have traveled in this course? What have you discovered afresh of faith, courage, compassion, solidarity and hope? If in a group, share this with your neighbor or maybe with the whole group. Conclude the course by saying together:

> **Risen Christ,**
> **you filled your disciples with boldness and fresh hope:**
> **strengthen us to proclaim your risen life**

and fill us with your peace,
to the glory of God the Father.

Bibliography

Ateek, Naim. *Contemporary Way of the Cross*. Jerusalem: Sabeel Ecumenical Liberation Centre, 2005.

Cunningham, Erin. "Ancient Gaza Roadway Still a Vital Resource", *The National*, 2010-03-10.

Dorotheos of Gaza, *Discourses and Sayings*. Translated by Eric P. Wheeler. Kalamazoo, Michigan: Cistercian, 1977.

Freyne, Sean. *Jesus, A Jewish Galilean: A New Reading of the Jesus-Story.* London: T & T Clark, 2004.

Horsley, Richard A. *Archaeology, History and Society in Galilee: the Social Context of Jesus and the Rabbis.* Valley Forge: Trinity International, 1995.

Lee, S. H. *From a Liminal Place: an Asian American Theology.* Minneapolis Fortress, 2010.

Mayes, Andrew D. *Holy Land? Challenging Questions from the Biblical Landscape.* London: SPCK, 2012.

———. *Beyond the Edge: Spiritual Transitions for Adventurous Souls.* London: SPCK, 2013.

———. *Gateways to the Divine: Transformative Pathways of Prayer from the Holy City of Jerusalem.* Oregon: Wipf and Stock, 2020.

Morton, Henry V. *In the Steps of the Master.* New York: Dodd, Mead & Co, 1935.

Moschos, John. *The Spiritual Meadow.* Translated by John Wortley. Kalamazoo, Michigan: Cistercian, 1992.

Thiede, Carsten Peter. *The Emmaus Mystery: Discovering Evidence for the Risen Christ.* London: Continuum, 2005.

Tolan, Sandy. *The Lemon Tree: An Arab, A Jew, and the Heart of the Middle East.* New York: Bloomsbury, 2006.

Vere, Monro. *A Summer Ramble in Syria, Vol. 1.* London: Richard Bentley, 1835.

Vivian, Tim. *Journeying Into God: Seven Early Monastic Lives.* Minneapolis: Fortress, 1996.

Zion, Ben Ilan. "Route 60: the deadly road that is the West Bank's lifeline". https://www.ft.com/content/8ba729f6-141c-11e9-a581-4ff78404524e January 24 2019.